Free-From Desserts

Free-From Desserts

PIES, PUDDINGS & ICE CREAMS ALL
WITHOUT DAIRY, WHEAT & GLUTEN

Julia Thomas

Quadrille
PUBLISHING

PHOTOGRAPHY BY ANDREW MONTGOMERY

FOR THE
WONDERFUL
RAINES: YOUR
FRIENDSHIP
MEANS THE
WORLD TO ME

X

Contents

INTRODUCTION 6

INGREDIENTS & EQUIPMENT 8

PASTRY 14

PIES & TARTS 22

TRADITIONAL PUDDINGS 54

CHILLED DESSERTS 84

ICE CREAMS & SORBETS 116

CREAMS & SAUCES 136

INDEX 156

Introduction

I wanted to call this book Not Another Lemon Sorbet, *which is probably a little unkind to lemon sorbets, but all too often they are the only dairy-, wheat- and gluten-free dessert on offer, and to a passionate pudding lover like me that is so disappointing. In fact, over the past 10 years I have spent an inordinate amount of time at dinner parties coveting my neighbour's pudding, watching with envy as they sink their spoon into some wonderfully wicked concoction…*

Maybe it's a generational thing, but as children my sister and I had a homemade pudding every day, and the puddings of my childhood are still some of my favourites today: steamed syrup sponge, jam roly-poly, apple pie, rhubarb crumble, raspberry ripple ice cream and the ubiquitous trifle. However, as I grew older and culinary fashions changed, so did my pudding choices. But it wasn't until I started writing this book that I realised I associated various periods in my life with the puddings I ate; a bit like certain perfumes or music, they transport me back to an earlier time!

In my early twenties I found myself working in the City as a recruitment consultant, not a job I was very good at (not pushy enough, I was reliably informed). To cheer myself up, every afternoon I would pop into the sandwich bar beneath my office and treat myself to a slice of Manhattan cheesecake. It was creamy and sweet and topped with a layer of cherry compote, and I loved it so much I must have eaten hundreds of slices. Then in my early thirties I discovered the joys of crema catalana, the Spanish version of crème brûlée. I can still remember the evening a foodie friend and I tried a new tapas bar in East London – all the dishes were delicious, but we out-did ourselves with three bowls each of the most mouth-watering crema catalana, a truly unforgettable moment.

In my late thirties I left the City and its wonderful restaurants and moved to rural Herefordshire. Not somewhere you would necessarily associate with fine dining, but luckily for me a quick hop over the Welsh border found me enjoying the delights of tiramisù at the legendary Walnut Tree in Abergavenny, and shortly thereafter Stephen Bull returned to his roots and opened a gastropub just outside Ross-on-Wye, where more delicious puddings awaited.

Disaster struck in my early forties when, newly pregnant, I was diagnosed with breast cancer. Whilst I gratefully accepted every treatment on offer, I also wanted to help myself, so after being introduced to Professor Jane Plant and reading her book *Your Life in Your Hands*, I decided to cut dairy from my diet. And so the next chapter of my culinary journey began. If we ate out, puddings were unfortunately off the menu, and if we went to friends, I might be offered a fruit salad or lemon sorbet. This isn't a criticism of friends, it was just that everyone cooked and baked with wheat flour, butter and cream. No one, and I include myself in this, realised there was any other option.

Of course I now know that I'm not alone in my desire for delicious dairy-, wheat- and gluten-free food, since Britain's 'free-from' food sector has seen meteoric growth in the last few years, with an increase of 50% in the last two years alone. Research shows that between 20 and 30% of the population believe they have a food intolerance, 2% have a diagnosed allergy and more people are making healthier lifestyle choices; that's an awful lot of people. This rapid and sustained growth means that there are now many more 'free-from' products available for us to choose from. At the moment I am having fun experimenting with coconut milk yoghurts, whilst my son Charlie regularly chooses to eat my 'free-from' alternatives, even though he doesn't need to.

Sadly, whilst we may never return to the days of my childhood when puddings were the norm rather than the exception, I do believe it's good for the soul to indulge in the occasional treat, and what better way to put a smile on the face of those you love than with a delicious homemade dessert. In our house sweet treats are normally reserved for the weekend and I'm quite sure one of the highlights of my nine-year-old son Charlie's weekend is sitting at the breakfast table on a Saturday morning planning how many puddings he can make and eat in two days!

For me, being in my kitchen is where I am happiest. Puddings are my passion and I absolutely adore testing and perfecting my recipes, making sure they are easy to follow and, most importantly, delicious to eat. Luckily for me Charlie and John – my cream- and butter-loving husband – happily help with the tasting, and since both delight in offering constructive criticism I know every single recipe in the book works! I have tried to include recipes for all occasions; some are quick and great for school night treats, and some are more sophisticated and make wonderful dinner party extravaganzas – but none are difficult. Just follow my instructions and you will soon be enjoying the kind of indulgent puddings you thought you had said good-bye to forever, puddings that everyone will want to share.

Ingredients

The following pages contain information on the dairy-, wheat- and gluten-free ingredients I use in my cooking, as well as those ingredients I consider important for delivering taste and flavour. You will find many of these ingredients lurking in the back of your cupboard, but some will be completely new to you; don't worry, they aren't difficult to use and most can be bought from the main supermarkets and good health food shops. And just in case you were wondering, all the recipes in this book work equally well with butter and wheat flours.

ALCOHOL

I don't keep a huge drinks cupboard, but there are a few bottles I always have to hand because they work so well in a wide range of recipes: brandy, dark rum, Frangelico, Grand Marnier or Cointreau, and a coffee liqueur such as Kahlúa. Always try to buy the best you can afford – after all, you may decide to drink them!

BAKING POWDER

Not all brands of this leavening agent are gluten-free, so check the ingredients label. I use Barkat and Dr Oetker gluten-free baking powder – both available in all the main supermarkets. Baking powder deteriorates over time, so check the use-by date.

BICARBONATE OF SODA

A leavening agent that doesn't include gluten and is commonly used in recipes together with acidic ingredients such as lemon juice or natural cocoa powder. Again, make sure you check the use-by date as it does deteriorate over time.

CHOCOLATE

As always, my favourite ingredient!

DARK CHOCOLATE – I use Plamil organic 60% drops for cooking.

MILK CHOCOLATE – I use Plamil drops for cooking.

WHITE CHOCOLATE – Melting dairy-free white chocolate has always been a bit of a challenge, but since I discovered Mortimer dairy-free white couverture powder, making ice cream and baking has become a doddle. When I decorate or sprinkle desserts with chocolate curls or gratings, I use chocolate bars. You can buy dairy-free chocolate bars from most good health food shops and all the main supermarkets stock the Kinnerton brand in the 'free-from' section.

The chocolate drops can be bought directly from Plamil, and the white chocolate powder from the online health and special diet store goodnessdirect.co.uk.

COCOA POWDER

Not to be confused with drinking chocolate, which contains sugar and milk. Cocoa powder makes the most wonderful chocolate sauce, is inexpensive and dairy- and gluten-free. Scientists also believe its potent antioxidants are good for our hearts, reduce blood pressure and could possibly prevent cancer. I use the Fairtrade, 100% organic brand Food Thoughts, which can be found in all the main supermarkets.

COCONUT

Coconut is an amazing fruit that has long been regarded as a superfood, and quite rightly so as it is high in omega-3 fatty acids, packed full of vitamins, minerals, antioxidants, electrolytes, fibre and saturated fats that help our body to burn fat, boost energy and increase good cholesterol. For those of us on a dairy-free diet, coconut provides a delicious and healthy alternative to dairy products.

OIL – I use Biona coconut oil and coconut butter in my baking as a replacement for other oils and butter, but it is expensive so I tend to use it in conjunction with other dairy-free products.

CANNED MILK – Coconut milk found in cans in the supermarket is not the watery liquid from inside the coconut but a mixture of the rich flesh and coconut water. Canned coconut milk contains about 17% fat. I keep these cans in the fridge so when the liquid and fatty cream separate I can scoop out the cream and whisk it into soft peaks. I use Waitrose Organic or M&S; you can use other brands but they don't whip up quite so successfully.

CARTON MILK – This is far less creamy, doesn't really taste of coconut and is sold in cartons alongside soya, rice and oat milk. I use Koko brand, which is sold in all the main supermarkets.

CREAM – Coconut cream is sold in small tins or cartons and should not be confused with creamed coconut, which is sold as a hard block. Like the cream scooped off the top of the tinned milk, it can be whipped into soft peaks or used as a base for ice creams and custards. I use Waitrose Organic, M&S or Blue Dragon brand, available in all the main supermarkets.

YOGHURT – Delicious coconut milk yoghurt can be purchased from health food shops and online, but as yet isn't available from the main supermarkets.

EGGS

I use organic free-range eggs in all my recipes, and I always remove my eggs from the fridge at least 30 minutes before using them. Liquid content is really important in wheat- and gluten-free baking, so I've indicated in each recipe whether to use large or medium sized eggs. Salmonella in raw eggs is thankfully a rare occurrence these days, but it is still cause for concern in the very young, elderly, pregnant women or people who are already unwell. To minimise food safety risks, I use British Lion eggs that have been vaccinated for salmonella. I store them in the fridge and I always make sure I use them before the best-before date.

ESPRESSO

Espresso has a much bolder flavour than coffee, which is why I use it in my recipes. If you aren't lucky enough to have your own espresso maker then you can use espresso powder – I mix a heaped teaspoon of powder with 60ml boiling water.

FATS

DAIRY-FREE SPREADS – I use dairy-free sunflower spread as a replacement for butter in most of my cooking. It is free of GM ingredients, hydrogenated oils, artificial additives, emulsifiers, soya and gluten and, importantly, has 70% less saturated fat than butter. I use Pure Sunflower spread but a number of the big supermarkets have their own brand of 'free-from' spreads; please remember to check the ingredients labels.

COCOMEGA – An organic coconut spread from Biona that contains 21% coconut oil and rapeseed oil and can be used as a replacement for butter and instead of sunflower spreads.

COCONUT OIL – I use Biona coconut oil in my biscuit bases as it sets nice and firm when chilled.

STORK MARGARINE – The block margarine is dairy-free but the tub margarine contains buttermilk. I am more than happy to use the block margarine in my pastry recipes and in the biscuit bases of my cheesecakes.

VEGETABLE FATS – Are free from hydrogenated vegetable oil, E numbers, preservatives and colours, and I use them in my pastry. Equal quantities of sunflower spread and vegetable fat are in my opinion the best combination for crisp and flaky pastry. I use either Cooken, Trex or Flora White.

FLOURS

Time is such a valuable commodity these days and whilst I love baking from scratch I find it so much easier to buy my wheat- and gluten-free flours already blended. Moreover, they work beautifully in all my recipes. A wide selection of brands can now be bought from good health food shops and of course the main supermarkets. All the recipes in this book use either self-raising or plain flour, and it is vitally important you use the right flour for each recipe or your pudding will end up a complete disaster. I use Doves Farm or Orgran plain and self-raising flour blends. If you can't get self-raising flour, add 2 teaspoons gluten-free baking powder and ¼ teaspoon salt to 150g plain wheat- and gluten-free flour, mixing well to make sure everything is distributed.

FRUIT

Ideally fruit should be perfectly ripe and in season, so wherever possible I like to support my local growers.

MILK PRODUCTS

If you are allergic to dairy, have made a lifestyle choice to consume less animal fat or simply don't like the taste, there are lots of alternative products for you to choose from that are comparable to regular milk, cream, yoghurt and cheese.

MILK – Dairy-free milks are really easy to cook with. They are low in fat and are normally calcium-enriched, but always check the ingredients label. I use Alpro unsweetened soya milk for making custards and creamy desserts, because it is richer and thicker in texture, whilst I like using the carton coconut milk Koko elsewhere, but rice, almond or oat milk will work just as well. It's really down to personal taste.

CREAM – Because I love the taste of coconut I am happy to make my own cream from chilled coconut milk, or use cartons of coconut cream instead of single cream, but if you don't like the taste there are several single cream alternatives: Alpro soya single cream is available from all the main supermarkets and Isola rice cream is available from the online health and special diet store goodnessdirect.co.uk.

YOGHURT – When I am organised, I order Co-Yo or Bessant and Drury's natural flavoured coconut yoghurt from the online health and special diet company goodnessdirect.co.uk. Otherwise, I use Alpro natural soya yoghurt, which is relatively inexpensive and readily available in all the main supermarkets.

CREAM CHEESE – Dairy-free cream cheese is a soya-based alternative that works brilliantly in cheesecakes. The brand I use is Tofutti.

SOUR CREAM – Another soya-based alternative that works brilliantly in cheesecakes, baking and served on jacket potatoes! I use Tofutti brand.

NUTS

It is really important to remember that nuts do not improve with age, so unless you bake on a regular basis only buy them when you are planning to use them. I always toast my nuts before using them as it enhances their flavour and gives them a bit more crunch.

OATS

Although oats do not contain gluten, some people are sensitive to a similar protein called avenins. Oat products can be contaminated with wheat or barley, so it is important to use gluten-free oats which can be found in the main supermarkets and health food shops.

OIL

Naturally refined organic sunflower and vegetable oils are neutral-tasting and wonderful to cook with, whilst other oils such as hazelnut and walnut have a stronger flavour and are best used in small quantities.

SUET

This creates a wonderful lightness in steamed winter puddings, and adds a richness to Christmas mincemeat. I always use Community Foods suet which is vegetarian and dusted with rice flour, and can be purchased in health food shops and online from goodnessdirect. co.uk. If you are unable to find vegetarian wheat- and gluten-free suet, you can replace it with the same quantity of coarsely grated vegetable fat such as Trex, Cooken, Flora White, Crisco or Copha. Vegetable fat can be soft to work with, so I always pop a block into the freezer

and then grate it frozen before popping it back into the freezer for 15 minutes. Stir the grated fat into the mixture until only white flecks remain, cook and store as if using suet. The pudding will have a slightly different texture to suet pudding but it will still be light and delicious.

SUGAR AND OTHER SWEETENERS

Put simply, sugar is an edible, crystalline carbohydrate that comes in many different forms, all of which taste sweet. I use a variety of sugars and sweeteners in my baking; some I use for the depth of their flavour and some for their chemical qualities. In all but one instance (see granulated) I use unrefined sugars that haven't been extensively processed, and which retain nutrients such as phosphorous, iron, calcium, magnesium and potassium.

CASTER SUGAR – A small-grained sugar that blends well in sponges, pastry and meringues. Unrefined caster sugar is light brown in colour and has a light caramel flavour.

GRANULATED SUGAR – Only white refined granulated sugar can be used to successfully make caramel, as unrefined granulated sugar and raw sugars contain impurities that inhibit the process.

ICING SUGAR – Very fine in texture, I use icing sugar in some of my pastry recipes and my meringues.

MUSCOVADO SUGARS – Made from raw cane sugar, these vary in colour and flavour. Light muscovado has a lovely toffee flavour, whilst dark muscovado has a strong molasses taste.

DEMERARA SUGAR – Has larger crystals than other sugars. I sprinkle it on desserts for texture.

GOLDEN SYRUP – A wonderfully thick, amber-coloured treacle made from the process of refining sugar cane or sugar beet juice into sugar, and I particularly love to use it in warm winter puddings and my treacle tart.

HONEY – Nature's sweetener is made by bees collecting nectar from flowers, so the flavour of the honey depends on where the bees have collected their nectar. Although honey is unrefined, it is still a sugar and therefore high in calories, but it does contain traces of niacin, riboflavin, thiamin and Vitamin B6. I use runny or clear honey in my baking, as cloudy honey is much too viscous.

MAPLE SYRUP – This comes from the sap of maple trees. It is collected, filtered and then boiled down into very sweet syrup. It contains fewer calories than honey but is sweeter than cane sugar and contains trace minerals manganese and zinc. I love the flavour but only use it occasionally as it is expensive.

AGAVE NECTAR – Derived from several species of the agave plant, the juice is extracted from the core of the plant then filtered and heated to break the complex components into simple sugars. The filtered juice is then concentrated into a thin syrup. It is 1½ times sweeter than sugar and is often substituted for sugar or honey in baking. The syrups are sold as light, amber, dark or raw varieties. The light syrup has an almost neutral flavour whilst the amber and dark varieties have a strong caramel flavour. Many agave nectars consist of 70–90% fructose so should be used in moderation.

COCONUT PALM SUGAR – Made from the liquid nectar of the coconut blossom, this is rich in potassium, magnesium, zinc and iron as well as Vitamins B1, B2, B3 and B6. It has the same number of calories and carbohydrates as granulated sugar, is subtly sweet like brown sugar, with a lovely hint of caramel, dark in colour and more expensive than other unrefined sugars. I love to use it in recipes with strong flavours.

VANILLA

Real vanilla is a hand-pollinated orchid whose seed pod is fermented and cured to produce the expensive but much prized flavour. Although native to Mexico, it is now cultivated in tiny plantations in Madagascar, Tahiti and Indonesia. Vanilla is one of the most common flavours in baking and is often used in a food product alongside the primary flavour, the best example being baked chocolate goods.

VANILLA EXTRACT – An alcohol and water solution containing vanillin, an organic compound responsible for the flavour of vanilla. Vanilla pods are crushed in the solution until the flavour has been well infused, which allows maximum flavour to be extracted from a single pod. The most commonly available extract originates from Madagascar, is sweet in flavour with light floral overtones, and is the flavour we think of when thinking of vanilla. Store in a cool, dark place with the lid kept tightly screwed.

VANILLA PODS – The ultimate in flavour and scent, these are perfect for infusing custard and ice cream. Really good pods are plump and smooth and filled with thousands of little brown seeds. They are expensive but I think they are worth it. Re-use your pods by rinsing and drying them thoroughly, then burying them in a jar of sugar.

VANILLA PASTE – A great in-between option for those who love the look of vanilla seeds but find vanilla pods inconvenient and difficult to use. The paste is made by infusing vanilla pods in a thick, sweet syrup made with sugar, water and a natural thickener. The vanilla seeds are then scraped out of the pods and into the paste to create a product that is incredibly easy to use.

VANILLA ESSENCE – Vanilla was one of the first flavours to be synthetically manufactured, and today it is extracted from clove oil and waste material from the wood and paper industry. I find it has a slightly bitter aftertaste but lots of people don't notice.

XANTHAN GUM

This is the magic ingredient that mimics the elastic effects of gluten in wheat- and gluten-free baking. Xanthan is derived from the cell coat of a microorganism called xanthomonas campestris and is a natural ingredient, made from the fermentation of corn sugars, although all corn sugars are removed in the process. The flour blends I use already contain small amounts of the gum but adding a little more improves the end result. If using wheat flour, no xanthan gum is needed.

Equipment

You really don't need an exhaustive list of expensive equipment in order to start making delicious puddings. In fact, you can start with just the basics, a bit of improvisation and lots of imagination. Chilled creams and mousses look beautiful served in a mismatched collection of vintage glasses and coffee cups, baked puddings and crumbles look rustically wholesome cooked in inexpensive white enamel pie dishes, and children love ice cream served in nostalgic waxed paper tubs. The only bit of advice I would give you is when buying new kitchen equipment, buy the best you can afford because with a bit of luck and some tender loving care, it will last you a lifetime.

BAKING BEANS
I use ceramic baking beans when blind baking my pastry, but my mother always used uncooked dried pasta which worked just as well.

BAKING PARCHMENT
Not to be confused with greaseproof paper, this wonderful invention is great for lining tins and trays and for baking blind pastry cases.

BAKING SHEETS
I recommend having at least two that are heavy, flat and rigid, but do check they fit into your oven.

CAKE TINS
These come in a variety of shapes and sizes and can vary dramatically in quality. The recipes in this book use only a few different types, but it is important to use the size and shape called for in the recipe.
ROUND TINS – I use 20, 23 and 25cm loose-bottomed tins in this book, and even though they are non-stick I still grease and line them with baking parchment.
SPRINGFORM TINS – Necessary for delicate cheesecakes that can't be removed from their tin by flipping over.

CLINGFILM
Rolling out pastry between two flour-dusted sheets of clingfilm ensures you can roll it out to an even thickness without it sticking to your work surface.

ELECTRIC HAND MIXER
I love my electric mixer; it is light but powerful and enables me to gauge how my ingredients are coming together. If you prefer, you can of course use a free-standing mixer for most of the recipes.

FOOD PROCESSOR
Food processors are brilliant time savers and I wouldn't be without mine, but if you aren't careful they can over-process. If making pastry I use it to process the flour and fat until it resembles breadcrumbs, then I add the liquid by hand before gently bringing it together into a ball. I also use it to crumb biscuits, purée fruit and make breadcrumbs, but I don't use it to chop nuts as I find it doesn't do a very even job.

FREEZER
Invaluable for a busy cook, freezers are great for storing pre-prepared pastry, tart cases, ice cream, sponges, fruit and sauces, meaning no last-minute panic when friends arrive unexpectedly.

ICE CREAM MACHINE
I have a fairly inexpensive ice cream machine that has always worked brilliantly for me, and because I'm never sure when an ice cream mood will take me I store the churning container in my freezer. If, however, you feel like treating yourself you could buy a wonderful machine with a built-in refrigeration unit that makes the whole process almost painless. If you don't have a machine, don't despair as you can make ice cream and sorbet by freezing the mixture in a shallow plastic container. Once the mixture starts to freeze you need to beat it with enthusiasm either by hand or electric hand mixer, repeating every half hour until it becomes too hard to beat.

JAM JARS
It's always useful to have a collection of jars with screw-top lids for storing sauces, caramels and coulis. To sterilise jars, see page 151.

KITCHEN BLOWTORCH

You don't really need one of these because you can caramelise sugar and brown meringues under the grill, but I love mine, it didn't cost much and I get a huge amount of satisfaction from using it!

MEASURING JUGS

To measure liquids I use a Pyrex heatproof jug that measures in metric and imperial.

MEASURING SPOONS

I find a set of measuring spoons essential – after all, a teaspoon in my drawer might not be the same size as the one in yours!

MIXING BOWLS

Because baking often requires the use of many bowls at the same time, I have a collection of glass bowls as well as lightweight stainless steel ones, all with rounded bases so I can reach all the mixture with my spatula, whisk or spoon.

PALETTE KNIFE

With its flexible blade and rounded end, this is the perfect tool for smoothing and spreading.

PASTRY BRUSHES

Perfect for greasing tins, applying glazes, and egg washing pastry. You can buy inexpensive soft bristled brushes which can be thrown away when they start to shed hairs, or silicon brushes in an array of vibrant colours.

PASTRY NOZZLE

Nozzles can be metal or plastic and are used with a piping bag. I keep a selection of sizes, but in this book I use the 1.5cm plain and fluted nozzles for piping meringue and sponge fingers.

PIE DISHES

Ceramic pie dishes are perfect for crumbles, as they look good straight from the oven.

PUDDING BASINS

An absolute must for steamed puddings. I inherited a range of sizes from my mother: the smallest is 1 litre and the largest 2.5 litres. They aren't very expensive and can be used as mixing bowls when needed.

RAMEKINS

The dictionary definition of a ramekin is 'a small dish for baking and serving an individual portion of food'. I have a set of eight in two different sizes, 110ml and 160ml, and they are perfect for individual crumbles, crème caramels and mousses.

ROLLING PIN

I use a long wooden rolling pin with no handles.

SAUCEPANS AND FRYING PANS

I have a really good set of stainless steel saucepans that aren't too heavy, cook evenly and have handles that don't heat up. It's worth investing in a good set that will last you for years, as cheap ones just don't last. If you like tarte Tatin, it's useful to have at least one ovenproof frying pan.

SCALES

Successful baking requires a good set of scales, but they don't need to be expensive. I use battery operated digital scales that measure weights as well as volumes in metric and imperial.

TART TINS

I use metal tins with shallow, fluted sides and removable bases, in three sizes: 20, 23 and 25cm. If you prefer straight and smooth sides, you will need to use a tart ring with no base, set on a greased and floured baking sheet.

TARTLET TINS

These are small metal tins with fluted sides and removable bases. If you prefer a shallow tart, then use a tin depth of 2cm but if you want a good, deep filling use a depth of 3cm. I love using a mixture of round and rectangular tins, just to ring the changes a bit.

THERMOMETERS

I strongly recommend you check the temperature of your oven with an inexpensive oven thermometer, as there is a very good chance your oven will cook at a different temperature to mine, in which case if necessary you can adjust the cooking times recommended in this book.

TIMERS

Timing is critical in baking, and as I know how easy it is to get distracted, I always set my trusty digital timer, then if I'm not around to rescue something, with any luck someone else will be!

WHISKS

Balloon whisks are great for getting air into a mixture without over-beating. I only ever use a metal one as silicone whisks can retain oil, which could be disastrous if whipping egg whites!

Pastry Tips & Techniques

There's something quite magical about pastry even though it's just a mix of flour, fat and a little liquid, and the same is true even if you don't use dairy, wheat or gluten. If you love light, flaky pastry, it really is worth the effort to make it by hand. Just remember that baking should be a real pleasure, so if you've never made pastry before, or tried and been disappointed, these general tips and techniques should help. The pastry recipes themselves are on pages 16–21.

If, like me, you have warm hands, then using a food processor to rub the flour into the fat is the only sensible option. If you don't have a food processor, I find rinsing my hands under the cold tap before I start really helps.

Make double the quantity of pastry needed and freeze the extra for later use. This saves time and effort in the long term.

Always read the recipe through before starting, and follow my instructions.

Make sure you have the right ingredients and weigh everything precisely.

Bake pastry in metal tins – they conduct the heat much better than ceramic dishes.

Keep everything very, very cold.

If using a food processor to rub the flour into the fat, only pulse for a couple of minutes otherwise, the dough will start coming together. Then transfer the pastry dough to a bowl.

If rubbing in by hand, use just your fingertips, otherwise the heat from your hands will start to melt the fat.

Add liquid gradually and toss rather than stir the mixture with a round-bladed knife – you want the dough to clump together loosely.

Bring the pastry together quickly using the heel of your hand, and don't knead it.

Flatten the pastry into a disc before wrapping it in clingfilm – it will be much easier to roll out than a round ball.

Chill the pastry in the fridge for a minimum of 1 hour, but preferably overnight; this keeps the fat cold and prevents it from melting and being absorbed into the flour.

Roll the pastry out between 2 large sheets of lightly floured clingfilm to about 3mm thick; turn the pastry by a quarter turn at each roll to ensure even rolling.

Don't stretch your pastry to fit your tin – it will just tear. Roll it out about 5cm larger than the tin.

Don't grease the tin, as there is enough fat in the pastry already.

Gently remove the top sheet of clingfilm, then lift the bottom sheet up and turn it over onto the tart tin. Gently press the pastry into place before peeling the clingfilm off. Trim the excess pastry by rolling the rolling pin across the top of the tin.

Repair any small splits with leftover pastry.

Lightly prick the base of the pastry case with a fork and place in the freezer for 30 minutes.

Always place your tin on a preheated baking sheet to bake it – this helps to prevent a soggy bottom.

Although confidence is key, please remember to relax and have fun!

SWEET SHORTCRUST PASTRY

I normally make at least double the quantity of sweet shortcrust pastry I actually need and freeze the rest. Most of my recipes require half the quantity of pastry this makes, so if you aren't going to bake again for a few days, wrap the remaining dough in clingfilm, pop it into a freezer bag and freeze. Always keep all pastry ingredients as cool as possible. If the fat starts to melt in the dough before it is cooked, your finished pastry will be tough.

Makes: 710g, enough to line two 20–23cm tart tins, 12 individual 10cm tins or two rectangular 36 x 12 x 2.5cm tins
Equipment: Food processor (optional)
Preparation time: 15 minutes
Chilling time: Minimum 1 hour, but preferably overnight
Freeze: Yes – for up to 3 months, but if you are freezing for longer than 2 months, add a drop of vinegar or lemon juice to the eggs, which will help to keep the pastry fresh

340g wheat- and gluten-free
   plain flour
2 tsp xanthan gum
¼ tsp salt
60g chilled vegetable lard, cubed
65g chilled dairy-free spread, cubed
125g unrefined caster sugar
2 large eggs plus 1 large yolk

Keep all your ingredients as cool as possible. If the fat starts to melt in the dough before it is cooked your finished pastry will be tough.

Sift the flour, xanthan gum and salt into a large bowl or the bowl of a food processor.

Add the chilled vegetable lard and dairy-free spread cubes and lightly rub in using your fingertips, or gently pulse in the food processor, until the mixture looks like fine breadcrumbs. Thirty seconds should be enough in the food processor and 1–2 minutes by hand.

If using a food processor, tip the mixture into a large mixing bowl.

Add the sugar, stir to combine, then make a well in the centre.

Beat the eggs and yolk together and pour into the well. Mix together lightly using a palette knife and then, using your hands, gently gather the pastry together to form a dough. Don't worry if it appears a bit dry; it will gradually come together, so don't be tempted to add more liquid, which would make the dough tough.

Handling the dough as lightly and as little as possible, so without kneading it, flatten it into a disc, wrap in clingfilm and chill in the fridge for at least 1 hour, but preferably overnight. If you are only going to use half, divide the dough into two, put one wrapped disc in a freezer bag and freeze.

TIP *To make lemon shortcrust pastry, add the finely grated zest of 1 lemon and juice of half to the eggs.*

HAZELNUT PASTRY

If you can't find blanched hazelnuts, use ones with their skins on, and when the nuts have cooled, rub them vigorously between two clean tea towels; the skins will come off easily and leave you with perfectly toasted nuts. Don't worry if you have a few stubborn ones; a bit of skin left on a nut won't affect the pastry.

Makes: 450g, enough to line a 20–23cm tart tin or eight individual 10cm tins
Equipment: Coffee grinder (ideally) or food processor
Preparation time: 15 minutes
Chilling time: Minimum 1 hour, but preferably overnight
Freeze: Yes – for up to 3 months, but if you are freezing for longer than 2 months, add a drop of vinegar or lemon juice to the eggs, which will help to keep the pastry fresh

30g blanched hazelnuts
35g unrefined caster sugar,
    plus ½ tsp to grind the nuts
220g wheat- and gluten-free
    plain flour
1 tsp xanthan gum
55g chilled vegetable lard, cubed
55g chilled dairy-free spread, cubed
1 large egg, beaten
1 tbsp ice-cold water
1 tsp vanilla extract or vanilla paste

Keep all your ingredients as cool as possible. If the fat starts to melt in the dough before it is cooked your finished pastry will be tough.

Preheat the oven to 190°C/170°C fan/Gas 5.

Spread the hazelnuts out on a baking tray and toast in the oven for 6–8 minutes, or until they become fragrant and start to turn brown. Remove from the oven, tip onto a plate and leave to cool.

Put the cooled nuts and the ½ teaspoon sugar into a coffee grinder or food processor and grind until fine (the sugar stops the nuts getting oily and clumping together).

Sift the flour, ground hazelnuts and xanthan gum into a large bowl or the bowl of a food processor.

Add the chilled vegetable lard and dairy-free spread cubes and lightly rub in using your fingertips, or gently pulse in the food processor, until the mixture looks like fine breadcrumbs. Thirty seconds should be enough in the food processor and 1–2 minutes by hand.

If using a food processor, tip the mixture into a large mixing bowl.

Add the sugar, stir to mix and make a well in the centre.

Mix the beaten egg with the cold water and vanilla extract and pour into the well. Mix together using your fingertips or a palette knife. Using your hands, gently gather the pastry together to form a dough; don't worry if it isn't smooth and you have a few dry bits left in the bottom of the bowl.

Handling the dough as lightly and as little as possible, so without kneading it, flatten it into a disc, wrap in clingfilm and chill in the fridge for at least 1 hour, but preferably overnight.

TIP *Because of their high fat content, nuts have a limited shelf life. Always store your nuts in airtight containers or freeze them in ziplock bags. Frozen nuts last up to a year and can be chopped and toasted straight from the freezer.*

PATE SUCREE

This is a classic French, sweet shortcrust pastry, traditionally made directly on a work surface and using only fingertips. I get into a dreadful mess making it this way, and so use a food processor. This pastry uses egg yolks instead of whole eggs, and icing sugar instead of caster sugar, giving it a fine and slightly crumbly texture that is completely different to sweet shortcrust pastry. It is perfect for tartlets and fruit-filled flans.

Makes: 450g, enough to line a 20–23cm tart tin, eight individual 10cm tins or a rectangular 36 x 12 x 2.5cm tin
Equipment: Food processor (optional)
Preparation time: 15 minutes
Chilling time: Minimum 1 hour, but preferably overnight
Freeze: Yes – for up to 3 months, but if you are freezing for longer than 2 months, add a drop of vinegar or lemon juice to the eggs, which will help to keep the pastry fresh

225g wheat- and gluten-free
   plain flour
2 tsp xanthan gum
50g chilled vegetable lard, cubed
50g chilled dairy-free spread, cubed
50g unrefined icing sugar, sifted
2 large egg yolks, beaten
2 tbsp ice-cold water
2 tsp vanilla extract or vanilla paste

Keep all your ingredients as cool as possible. If the fat starts to melt in the dough before it is cooked your finished pastry will be tough.

Sift the flour and xanthan gum into a large bowl or the bowl of a food processor.

Add the chilled vegetable lard and dairy-free spread cubes and lightly rub in using your fingertips, or gently pulse in the food processor, until the mixture looks like fine breadcrumbs. Thirty seconds should be enough in the food processor and 1–2 minutes by hand.

If using a food processor, tip the mixture into a large mixing bowl.

Add the sifted icing sugar, stir to combine, then make a well in the centre of the ingredients.

Mix the beaten egg yolks with the cold water and vanilla extract and pour into the well. Mix together lightly using a palette knife. Using your hands, gently gather the pastry together to form a soft dough; don't be tempted to knead it.

Handling the dough as lightly and as little as possible, so without kneading it, flatten it into a disc, wrap in clingfilm and chill in the fridge for at least 1 hour, but preferably overnight.

CHOCOLATE PATE SUCREE

This pastry is the perfect partner for rich chocolate truffle centres, but I think it works equally well filled with vanilla or chocolate crème pâtissière, topped with seasonal fresh fruit and a lick of redcurrant glaze.

Makes: 400g, enough to line a 20–23cm tart tin or eight individual 10cm tins
Equipment: Food processor (optional)
Preparation time: 15 minutes
Chilling time: Minimum 1 hour, but preferably overnight
Freeze: Yes – for up to 3 months, but if you are freezing for longer than 2 months, add a drop of vinegar or lemon juice to the eggs, which will help to keep the pastry fresh

175g wheat- and gluten-free plain flour
25g cocoa powder
1 tsp xanthan gum
50g chilled vegetable lard, cubed
50g chilled dairy-free spread, cubed
50g unrefined icing sugar, sifted
1 medium egg yolk, beaten
4 tsp ice-cold water

Keep all your ingredients as cool as possible. If the fat starts to melt in the dough before it is cooked your finished pastry will be tough.

Sift the flour, cocoa powder and xanthan gum into a large bowl or the bowl of a food processor.

Add the chilled vegetable lard and dairy-free spread cubes and lightly rub in using your fingertips, or gently pulse in the food processor, until the mixture looks like fine breadcrumbs. Thirty seconds should be enough in the food processor and 1–2 minutes by hand.

If using a food processor, tip the mixture into a large mixing bowl.

Add the icing sugar, stir, then make a well in the centre.

Mix the beaten egg yolk with the cold water and pour into the well. Mix together using your fingertips or a palette knife. Using your hands, gently gather the pastry together to form a dough.

Handling the dough as lightly and as little as possible, so without kneading it, flatten into a disc, wrap in clingfilm or baking parchment and chill in the fridge for at least 1 hour, but preferably overnight.

ALMOND PASTRY

This is a lovely alternative to sweet shortcrust pastry, and works exceptionally well with my Macaroon and Toasted Almond Mincemeat Tartlets (page 29). It has a completely different texture to other pastries and is very easy to make, although it needs to be handled gently.

Makes: 430g, enough to line a 20–23cm tart tin, eight individual 10cm tins, 18 mini tart tins or a rectangular 36 x 12 x 2.5cm tin
Equipment: Food processor (optional)
Preparation time: 15 minutes
Chilling time: Minimum 2 hours, but preferably overnight
Freeze: Yes – for up to 3 months, but if you are freezing for longer than 2 months, add a drop of vinegar or lemon juice to the eggs, which will help to keep the pastry fresh

170g wheat- and gluten-free plain flour
1 tsp xanthan gum
50g chilled vegetable lard, cubed
50g chilled dairy-free spread, cubed
60g ground almonds
50g unrefined icing sugar, sifted
2 large egg yolks
2 tsp vanilla extract or vanilla paste

Keep all your ingredients as cool as possible. If the fat starts to melt in the dough before it is cooked your finished pastry will be tough.

Sift the flour and xanthan gum into a large bowl or the bowl of a food processor.

Add the chilled vegetable lard and dairy-free spread cubes and lightly rub in using your fingertips, or gently pulse in the food processor, until the mixture looks like fine breadcrumbs. Thirty seconds should be enough in the food processor and 1–2 minutes by hand.

If using a food processor, tip the mixture into a large mixing bowl.

Add the ground almonds and icing sugar and stir to combine, then make a well in the centre.

Beat the egg yolks and vanilla extract or paste together and pour into the well. Mix together lightly using a palette knife. Using your hands, gently gather the pastry together to form a very soft dough (it is meant to be a completely different texture to sweet shortcrust pastry).

Handling the dough as lightly and as little as possible, so without kneading it, flatten it into a disc, wrap in clingfilm and chill in the fridge for at least 2 hours, but preferably overnight.

ORANGE FLOWER WATER PASTRY

Sometimes changing the flavour of your pastry can revitalise an old and trusted recipe, and this wonderfully exotic pastry can lend a bit of added zest to fruit tarts. It also makes a glorious base to my Rhubarb and Custard Tartlets (page 28). It's a delicate pastry, so handle with care and don't try to roll it out too thinly.

Makes: 500g, enough to line a 20–23cm tart tin, eight individual 10cm tins or a rectangular 36 x 12 x 2.5cm tin
Equipment: Food processor (optional); electric hand mixer
Preparation time: 15 minutes
Chilling time: Minimum 1 hour, but preferably overnight
Freeze: Yes – for up to 3 months, but if you are freezing for longer than 2 months, add a drop of vinegar or lemon juice to the eggs, which will help to keep the pastry fresh

250g wheat- and gluten-free plain flour
1 tsp xanthan gum
75g chilled vegetable lard, cubed
75g chilled dairy-free spread
75g icing sugar, sifted
Finely grated zest of 1 large orange
2 large egg yolks, beaten
1 tsp orange flower water

Keep all your ingredients as cool as possible. If the fat starts to melt in the dough before it is cooked your finished pastry will be tough.

Sift the flour and xanthan gum into a large bowl or the bowl of a food processor.

Add the chilled vegetable lard cubes and lightly rub in using your fingertips, or gently pulse in the food processor, until the mixture looks like fine breadcrumbs. Thirty seconds should be enough in the food processor or 1–2 minutes by hand.

Using an electric hand mixer, beat the dairy-free spread, icing sugar, orange zest, egg yolks and orange flower water together in a large bowl.

Add the flour mixture and mix with a palette knife, then start bringing the pastry together using your fingertips.

Handling the dough as lightly as possible, so without kneading it, flatten it into a disc, wrap in clingfilm and chill in the fridge for at least 1 hour, but preferably overnight.

TIP *You can find orange flower water in the baking section of most supermarkets, but don't confuse it with orange extract, which is an oil and a completely different flavour.*

FROM MY MUCH-LOVED TARTE TATIN RECIPE,
TO THE SMALL BUT PERFECTLY FORMED
RASPBERRY TARTLETS AND THE SIMPLE BUT
NO-LESS-DELICIOUS GOOSEBERRY GALETTE,
THESE ARE JUST SOME OF MY FAMILY'S
FAVOURITE PIE AND TART RECIPES – I WANT
TO SHARE THEM ALL WITH YOU.

Pies & Tarts

TARTE TATIN

I make no apologies for adoring a good tarte Tatin and years ago I travelled through France happily trying to find the perfect one. I might not eat wheat or dairy these days, but that doesn't mean I don't still love this French classic. I have spent hours on my research and I think my recipe is now pretty near perfect. Try not to eat the tarte as soon as it comes out of the oven; leaving it to cool for a minimum of an hour allows the caramel to thicken and become stickier.

Serves: 8–10
Equipment: Food processor (optional); 23cm heavy-based, ovenproof frying pan or specialist Tarte Tatin pan
Preparation time: Approx. 30 minutes plus 24 hours chilling and 30 minutes cooling
Cooking time: Approx. 1 hour
Freeze: No

6–7 Cox's apples, depending on size
1 quantity Pâte Sucrée (page 18)
70ml water
150g unrefined granulated sugar
50ml coconut cream
Pinch of salt

TIP *I use Cox's Orange Pippins, but you could use Braeburn or Crimson Cox. Whilst I love the sharper taste of the Granny Smith, they release a lot more juice during cooking, which can make your caramel too runny.*

Peel, core and halve the apples, then place them on a large plate and chill them in the fridge, uncovered, for 24 hours.

Make the pastry, wrap in clingfilm and chill in the fridge for a minimum of 1 hour, or overnight if possible.

Pour the water into your frying pan or Tarte Tatin pan and sprinkle the granulated sugar over it. Leave it to dissolve for a couple of minutes.

Cook the sugar and water over a medium heat, stirring occasionally with a wooden spoon, until it turns into lovely golden caramel, approximately 15 minutes. Remove from the heat and very gently add the coconut cream and salt. Stir gently to combine.

Remove the apples from the fridge and arrange them, round side down, in the pan, being careful not to touch the hot caramel with your fingers. It is important to pack the apples in as tightly as possible; you may need to cut some of them into smaller pieces to fill in any gaps.

Place the pan back on the heat for a further 10–15 minutes or until the apples are nicely covered with hot caramel.

Remove the pan from the heat for 30 minutes. Meanwhile, preheat the oven to 200°C/ 180°C fan/Gas 6.

Roll the pastry out into a circle slightly larger than your pan and 5mm thick (see page 14). Refrigerate again until the apples have cooled.

Once the apples have cooled, place the pastry circle on top of the pan and carefully tuck the edge inside the pan around the apples.

Bake the tarte for 30 minutes or until the pastry is golden in colour.

Remove the tarte from the oven and leave to cool in the pan for 1 hour.

Place a plate slightly larger than your pan on top of it and very carefully, using oven gloves, invert the tarte onto the plate. Be careful, as the caramel may run off.

Serve warm with a jug of Coconut Cream or a scoop of Madagascan Vanilla Ice Cream.

PEAR, CHOCOLATE AND HAZELNUT TART

Who could fail to love the sweetness of pears, the crunch of hazelnuts and the richness of chocolate here? I like to make the pastry, poached pears and crème pâtissière the day before.

Serves: 8–10 **Equipment:** Rectangular 36 x 12 x 2.5cm loose-bottomed tart tin; food processor (optional)
Preparation time: 1 hour plus cooling and chilling overnight **Cooking time:** Approx. 50 minutes **Freeze:** No

---

½ quantity Sweet Shortcrust Pastry
    (page 16)
30g blanched hazelnuts
75g best-quality (60% cocoa) dark,
    dairy-free chocolate

Poached Pears
1 litre water
265g unrefined granulated sugar
1 vanilla pod, split lengthways
4 large or 8 small firm but ripe pears
    (I use Conference), peeled, halved
    and neatly cored

Crème Pâtissière Filling
1 quantity Crème Pâtissière
    (page 146)
1 tbsp Frangelico

TIP Replace the sugar in the syrup with 320g runny honey or poach the pears in a mixture of 500ml water and 500ml sparkling white wine.

Put the water and sugar in a large saucepan. Scrape out the vanilla seeds and add with the pod to the pan. Gradually bring to the boil, stirring until the sugar dissolves. Carefully add the halved pears and cover them with a circle of baking parchment, with a small hole cut in the middle to allow the steam to escape. Keep the liquid at a low boil and simmer for 15–25 minutes or until cooked.

Remove from the heat and allow the pears and liquid to completely cool in the pan. Put in a bowl, cover and chill in the fridge overnight.

When you've made the pastry, wrap in clingfilm and rest it in the fridge for at least 1 hour, or overnight if possible.

Roll out the chilled pastry and use to line the tin (see page 14). Lightly prick the base with a fork and freeze for 30 minutes. Preheat the oven to 190°C/170°C fan/Gas 5 and put in a baking sheet to heat. Line the chilled pastry case with baking parchment and ceramic beans. Blind bake on the hot baking sheet for 15 minutes or until the pastry is starting to turn golden. Remove the parchment and beans, then return to the oven for 10 minutes or until golden. Set aside to cool.

Scatter the hazelnuts on a baking sheet and toast in the oven for 6–8 minutes. Remove from the oven, allow to cool, then roughly chop. Drain and dry the chilled pears (don't waste the syrup – keep it for another recipe).

Melt the chocolate in a heatproof bowl set over a pan of barely simmering water, making sure the base of the bowl doesn't touch the water. Spoon most of the chocolate, saving some to decorate, into the cold pastry case. Using a pastry brush, gently paint the sides and base. Cool for 10 minutes, then refrigerate on a baking sheet.

Whisk the Frangelico into the crème pâtissière as soon as it is off the heat. Pour into a bowl and cover the surface with clingfilm, to prevent a skin from forming. Leave to cool, then chill in the fridge until needed.

To assemble, spoon the crème pâtissière into the pastry case and spread evenly. Arrange the pears, cut side down, on top. Gently reheat the reserved chocolate and drizzle over the pears. Sprinkle the toasted hazelnuts on top. Refrigerate for a couple of hours before serving.

RHUBARB AND CUSTARD TARTLETS

It might be trendy these days to pair rhubarb with exotic flavours such as cardamom or saffron, but personally I think vanilla is still rhubarb's best friend. Early February brings the first batch of Yorkshire forced rhubarb, with its jewel-like colour and tender young stems; it requires only a light poaching, and pairing it with custard in a dainty tartlet is a heavenly way of celebrating the arrival of spring.

Serves: 8
Equipment: Eight 10cm loose-bottomed, deep tartlet tins; food processor (optional); electric hand mixer
Preparation time: 1 hour plus minimum 1½ hours chilling
Cooking time: 45 minutes
Freeze: No

1 quantity Orange Flower Water Pastry (page 21)
1 egg, beaten with 1 tbsp soya, rice, almond or coconut milk

Filling
250g forced rhubarb, cut into 2.5cm pieces
125ml water
250g unrefined caster sugar
3 large eggs
1 tsp vanilla paste
250ml dairy-free sour cream, at room temperature

TIP *If you can't get forced rhubarb, then maincrop will be fine. The stalks won't be quite as pink and they will be thicker, so chop into small pieces and poach for slightly longer.*

Make the pastry, wrap in clingfilm and chill in the fridge for a minimum of 1 hour, or overnight if possible.

Divide the chilled pastry roughly into 8 pieces. Roll out one piece to fit and line a tartlet tin (see page 14), keeping the remaining pieces in the fridge as you work. Lightly prick the base with a fork.

Repeat the process for the remaining 7 tartlet tins and transfer to the freezer to chill for 30 minutes. Meanwhile, preheat the oven to 190°C/170°C fan/Gas 5 and place a baking sheet in the oven to heat.

Line the pastry cases with baking parchment and ceramic beans and transfer to the hot baking sheet in the oven. Blind bake for 15 minutes.

Remove from the oven and lift the parchment and ceramic beans out; take care, as they will be very hot. Brush the beaten egg and milk mixture over the pastry cases and return to the oven for a further 10 minutes, then set aside to cool. Reduce the oven temperature to 180°C/160°C fan/Gas 4.

Meanwhile, for the filling, put the rhubarb in a saucepan with the water and 50g of the sugar. Bring to the boil, then almost immediately remove from the heat; the rhubarb should be tender but not falling apart. Drain, reserving the liquid and setting the rhubarb aside, then return the liquid to the pan and bring to the boil. Simmer over a medium heat for 10–15 minutes or until reduced to a thick syrup. Remove from the heat and leave to cool.

Put the eggs, remaining sugar and vanilla paste into a large bowl and beat with an electric hand mixer for a couple of minutes until thick and creamy. Put the sour cream into a small bowl and lightly whisk with the hand mixer or a wooden spoon before adding to the egg and sugar mixture. Beat again until combined.

Arrange the rhubarb in the base of each tartlet case and fill each case with the custard mixture. Cook in the oven for 20 minutes or until the custard has turned a lovely golden colour and is firm to a light touch.

Remove from the oven and leave to cool for 15 minutes. Serve with a scoop of ice cream and a drizzle of the reserved rhubarb syrup.

MACAROON AND TOASTED ALMOND MINCEMEAT TARTLETS

To quote the 1970s band Wizard: 'I wish it could be Christmas every day', then I could happily justify eating one of these little beauties on a daily basis. I make and use my own mincemeat (page 151), which is less sweet than shop-bought, but if you are using shop-bought, buy a luxury brand and stir in a little booze or grated orange zest, just to make it a bit more special.

Serves: 8
Equipment: Eight 10cm shallow tartlet tins; food processor (optional); electric hand mixer
Preparation time: 30 minutes plus minimum 2½ hours chilling
Cooking time: 25–30 minutes
Freeze: Yes – for up to 6 months. Cool completely, then open freeze before wrapping in clingfilm or foil. Defrost in the fridge overnight and then warm through in a 180°C/160°C fan/Gas 4 oven for 10–15 minutes

1 quantity Almond Pastry (page 20)
480g best-quality mincemeat

Macaroon Topping
175g unrefined caster sugar
175g ground almonds
75g flaked almonds
3 large egg whites
½ tsp almond extract

Make the pastry, wrap in clingfilm and chill in the fridge for a minimum of 2 hours, or overnight if possible.

Divide the chilled pastry roughly into 8 pieces. Roll out one piece to fit and line a tartlet tin (see page 14), keeping the remaining pieces in the fridge as you work. Lightly prick the base with a fork.

Repeat the process for the remaining 7 tart tins and transfer to the freezer to chill for 30 minutes. Meanwhile, preheat the oven to 190°C/170°C fan/Gas 5 and place a baking sheet in the oven to heat.

To make the topping, put the sugar, ground almonds and 25g of the flaked almonds into a large mixing bowl and stir to combine.

In a separate bowl, beat the egg whites until stiff using an electric hand mixer. Stir the beaten egg whites and almond extract into the dry ingredients to form a stiff mixture.

Spoon about 50g mincemeat into each chilled pastry case, then spoon 50g macaroon mixture on top of each. Using a round-bladed knife, smooth it to the edges of the tarts, ensuring the mincemeat is covered. Sprinkle the tops with the remaining flaked almonds.

Place the tartlets on the hot baking sheet in the oven and bake for 25–30 minutes or until the topping is firm and a lovely golden colour.

Remove from the oven and leave to cool. The tarts are delicious served warm with a scoop of ice cream.

TIP *This recipe also makes 18 mince pies made in a shallow bun tin rather than the deeper muffin or cupcake tin.*

MY TREACLE TART

Whilst I have very happy childhood memories of school treacle tart and I'm sure at the time it was delicious, with age I have become rather more particular about certain elements of the recipe. It should definitely include some, but not too much, dark treacle otherwise it can't call itself a treacle tart. Lemon juice is really important to cut through the sweetness, and finally it should have a slightly chewy surface with a soft melt-in-the-mouth centre. This is my perfect treacle tart.

Serves: 8–10
Equipment: Rectangular 36 x 12 x 2.5cm loose-bottomed tart tin; food processor (optional)
Preparation time: 1 hour plus minimum 1½ hours chilling
Cooking time: Approx. 1 hour
Freeze: Yes – once cool, open freeze until solid, then wrap well in foil or clingfilm. Freeze for up to 6 months. Defrost overnight in the fridge. To serve hot, reheat at 180°C/160°C fan/Gas 4 for 15–20 minutes

½ quantity Sweet Shortcrust Pastry (page 16)
1 egg, beaten with 1 tbsp soya, rice, almond or coconut milk

Treacle Filling
60g dairy-free spread
450g golden syrup
25g dark treacle
2 tbsp coconut cream
1 tbsp lemon juice
¼ tsp salt
1 large egg plus 1 large yolk
70g white wheat- and gluten-free breadcrumbs
70g brown wheat- and gluten-free breadcrumbs

Make the pastry, wrap in clingfilm and chill in the fridge for at least 1 hour, or overnight if possible.

Roll out the chilled pastry to a rectangle slightly larger than the tin and 3mm thick (see page 14). Use to line the tart tin, lightly prick the base with a fork and chill in the freezer for 30 minutes. Meanwhile, preheat the oven to 190°C/170°C fan/Gas 5 and place a baking sheet in the oven to heat.

Line the chilled pastry case with baking parchment and ceramic beans. Blind bake on the hot baking sheet in the oven for 15 minutes or until the pastry is starting to turn golden. Remove from the oven and lift the parchment and ceramic beans out; take care, as they will be very hot.

Brush the beaten egg and milk mixture over the pastry case. Return to the oven for 10 minutes or until the pastry is a lovely golden colour. Set aside to cool.

Melt the dairy-free spread in a medium saucepan, then add the golden syrup and treacle to warm through; you don't need the mixture to be hot. Remove from the heat and stir in the coconut cream, lemon juice, salt, egg and egg yolk.

Mix the breadcrumbs together and sprinkle evenly over the base of the cooled pastry case.

Transfer the syrup mixture to a large jug and very carefully pour over the breadcrumbs, making sure they are all covered.

Return the tart to the oven and bake for 20 minutes, then reduce the oven temperature to 140°C/120°C fan/Gas 1 and bake for a further 15–20 minutes until the middle is set but still slightly wobbly.

Leave to cool before slicing and serving with Madagascan Vanilla Ice Cream or Coconut Cream.

TIP *If you don't have a rectangular tart tin, you can use a round 23cm loose-bottomed tart tin.*

PERFECT PECAN PIE

It was first thought that the French introduced pecan pie to New Orleans when they settled there in the early 1700s, but food historians have never been able to trace a recipe back further than 1940, so it's probably a fanciful theory. Whatever its history, pecan pie is now a firm favourite this side of the Atlantic as well, and is particularly popular with my nut-loving husband.

Serves: 8–10
Equipment: 23cm tart tin; food processor (optional)
Preparation time: 1 hour plus minimum 1½ hours chilling
Cooking time: Approx. 1¼ hours
Freeze: Yes – once cool, open freeze until solid, then wrap well in foil or clingfilm. Freeze for up to 6 months. Defrost overnight in the fridge. To serve hot, reheat at 180°C/160°C fan/Gas 4 for 15–20 minutes

½ quantity Sweet Shortcrust Pastry (page 16)
1 egg, beaten with 1 tbsp soya, rice, almond or coconut milk

Filling
125g pecan nuts
100g dark muscovado sugar
100ml maple syrup
85g dairy-free spread
200ml coconut cream
35g cornflour
3 large egg yolks
2 tbsp dark rum
¼ tsp salt

Make the pastry, wrap in clingfilm and chill in the fridge for at least 1 hour, or overnight if possible.

Roll out the chilled pastry into a rough circle slightly larger than the tin and 3mm thick (see page 14). Use to line the tart tin, lightly prick the base with a fork and chill in the freezer for 30 minutes. Meanwhile, preheat the oven to 190°C/170°C fan/Gas 5 and place a baking sheet in the oven to heat.

Line the pastry case with baking parchment and ceramic beans. Bake in the oven on the hot baking sheet for 15 minutes or until the pastry is starting to turn golden.

Remove the tart from the oven and lift the parchment and ceramic beans out; take care, as they will be very hot.

Brush the beaten egg and milk mixture over the pastry case. Return to the oven for 10 minutes or until the pastry is a lovely golden colour. Set aside to cool, and reduce the oven temperature to 180°C/160°C fan/Gas 4.

Spread the pecan nuts out on a baking sheet and toast in the oven for 6 minutes. Remove from the oven, tip onto a board and leave to cool a little before roughly chopping half of them.

Put the sugar, maple syrup, dairy-free spread and coconut cream in a heatproof bowl set over a pan of simmering water. Stir until everything has melted together, about 15 minutes.

Sprinkle the cornflour into the mixture and whisk until it thickens slightly, about 5 minutes. Remove from the heat and whisk in the egg yolks, rum, salt and the chopped pecan nuts.

Carefully pour the mixture into the pastry case. Place the remaining whole pecan nuts gently on the surface in a circular pattern.

Place on the baking sheet and bake for 45–50 minutes or until set on top. Serve warm with thick coconut cream or a scoop of ice cream.

GOOSEBERRY FRANGIPANE GALETTE

The layer of frangipane elevates this rustic French tart into something a bit special. The pastry, with its wonderfully crunchy sugar-coated crust, is supposed to be untidy, so it really doesn't matter if it isn't rolled out perfectly into a precise circle. I love gooseberries and have bags of them in my freezer, so this recipe provides a brilliant way for me to showcase them. If you find them too tart, just sprinkle a little more caster sugar over them before baking.

Serves: 6
Equipment: Food processor (optional); electric hand mixer
Preparation time: 30 minutes plus minimum 1½ hours chilling
Cooking time: 35–40 minutes
Freeze: No

½ quantity Sweet Shortcrust Pastry (page 16)

Filling
½ quantity Frangipane (page 150)
700g gooseberries, frozen or fresh, topped and tailed
75g unrefined caster sugar
1 large egg white, beaten
8 brown sugar cubes, crushed

TIP *You can substitute the gooseberries for 700g blackcurrants, reducing the sugar to 50g, or for 6 Cox's apples, peeled, cored and sliced, reducing the sugar to 60g. Almond Pastry (page 20) or Hazelnut Pastry (page 17) make great alternatives to the sweet shortcrust.*

Make the pastry, wrap in clingfilm and chill in the fridge for at least 1 hour, or overnight if possible.

Meanwhile, make the frangipane, cover and chill in the fridge until it's needed.

Put a baking sheet in the oven and preheat the oven to 180°C/160°C fan/Gas 4.

Place the chilled pastry on a sheet of clingfilm lightly dusted with flour. Place another sheet of clingfilm on top of the pastry and gently roll the pastry out into a circle, roughly 30cm in diameter and 3mm thick. You might need to pull the clingfilm taut after several rolls to ensure it doesn't get caught up in the pastry. Gently remove the top sheet of clingfilm, then lift the bottom sheet up and turn over gently onto a sheet of baking parchment.

Spoon the frangipane onto the pastry base and use a palette knife to spread it evenly over the pastry, leaving a 5cm border all around.

Pile the gooseberries over the frangipane filling, sprinkling the sugar in between the berries.

Turn in the 5cm border all the way round to form a ridged edge; it doesn't matter if it isn't neat, as a galette is meant to be informal.

Brush the pastry surface with the beaten egg white and sprinkle with the crushed sugar cubes.

Slide the galette, on its paper, onto the hot baking sheet in the oven and bake for 35–40 minutes, then leave to cool slightly before serving with a scoop of your favourite ice cream.

CHOCOLATE WALNUT TRUFFLE TARTLETS WITH CHOCOLATE AND GRAND MARNIER GLAZE

Be warned: these gorgeous little tartlets, with their crunchy chocolate bottoms, are totally addictive. One evening, I managed to eat three, and could probably have managed four if someone else hadn't already beaten me to it!

Serves: 8
Equipment: Eight 10cm loose-bottomed shallow tartlet tins; food processor (optional)
Preparation time: 1 hour plus minimum 1½ hours chilling
Cooking time: 25 minutes
Freeze: No

1 quantity Chocolate Pâte Sucrée (page 19)
60g best-quality (60% cocoa) dark, dairy-free chocolate, chopped

Filling
85g best-quality (60% cocoa) dark, dairy-free chocolate, chopped
15g dairy-free spread
110ml coconut cream
Pinch of salt
1 large egg plus 1 large yolk
50g walnuts, ground with ½ tsp unrefined caster sugar in a coffee grinder or food processor

Glaze
25g cocoa powder
35g unrefined caster sugar
25ml agave nectar
85ml water
1 tbsp Grand Marnier
20g best-quality (60% cocoa) dark, dairy-free chocolate, chopped

Make the pastry, wrap in clingfilm and chill in the fridge for a minimum of 2 hours, or overnight if possible.

Divide the chilled pastry roughly into 8 pieces. Roll out one piece to fit and line a tartlet tin (see page 14), keeping the remaining pieces in the fridge as you work. Lightly prick the base with a fork. Repeat the process for the remaining 7 tart tins and transfer to the freezer to chill for 30 minutes. Meanwhile, preheat the oven to 190°C/170°C fan/Gas 5 and place a baking sheet in the oven to heat. Blind bake the tartlets following the method on page 28. Leave to cool.

For the glaze, whisk the cocoa powder, sugar, agave nectar and water together in a heavy-based saucepan over a medium heat until the cocoa has dissolved, then bring to a gentle boil.

Remove the pan from the heat, stir in the Grand Marnier and add the chocolate, whisking until it has melted and the mixture is smooth and glossy. Place in the fridge to cool and thicken.

Melt the 60g chocolate in a heatproof bowl set over a saucepan of barely simmering water, making sure the base of the bowl doesn't touch the water.

Spoon ½ teaspoon of the melted chocolate into each cold pastry case and, using a pastry brush, gently paint up the sides and across the base of the cases. Leave to cool for 30 minutes, then chill in the fridge to set.

For the filling, put the 85g chocolate and dairy-free spread into a heatproof bowl. Bring the coconut cream to a low boil in a small, heavy-based pan, pour it over the chocolate and dairy-free spread and leave for 30 seconds before whisking to combine. Whisk in the salt, egg and yolk, then add the ground walnuts and stir to combine.

Pour the mixture into the cooled pastry cases, leaving a 2mm space at the top for the glaze, and return to the fridge for 2 hours or until the filling is firm to the touch.

Pour a thin layer of the chilled glaze over the filling in each tartlet and then return to the fridge to chill before serving with lashings of gently whipped Coconut Cream.

TARTE AU CITRON WITH CARAMELISED CRUST

Apparently, a perfect lemon tart is the hallmark of a great pastry chef, and I have to agree that this tart really does look the business. The caramelised crust not only adds a very pleasing crunch, it also lends the tart a degree of professionalism of which I must admit I am very proud.

Serves: 8–10
Equipment: 23cm tart tin; food processor (optional); electric hand mixer; cook's blowtorch (optional)
Preparation time: 30 minutes plus minimum 1½ hours chilling
Cooking time: Approx. 1 hour 25 minutes
Freeze: No

1 quantity Pâte Sucrée (page 18)
1 egg, beaten with 1 tbsp soya, rice, almond or coconut milk
Icing sugar, to dust

Filling

6 large eggs
175g unrefined caster sugar
Grated zest of 6 large lemons
275ml lemon juice (6–8 large lemons)
200ml coconut cream

Make the pastry, wrap in clingfilm and chill in the fridge for at least 1 hour, or overnight if possible.

Roll out the chilled pastry to a circle slightly larger than the tart tin and 3mm thick (see page 14). Use to line the tin, lightly prick the base with a fork and chill in the freezer for 30 minutes. Meanwhile, preheat the oven to 190°C/170°C fan/Gas 5 and place a baking sheet in the oven to heat up.

Line the pastry case with baking parchment and ceramic beans. Bake in the oven on the hot baking sheet for 15 minutes or until the pastry is starting to turn golden. Remove from the oven and lift the parchment and ceramic beans out; take care, as they will be very hot.

Brush the beaten egg and milk mixture over the pastry case. Return to the oven for 10 minutes or until the pastry is golden all over. Set aside to cool and reduce the oven temperature to 140°C/120°C fan/Gas 1.

Put the eggs and sugar for the filling into a large bowl and, using an electric hand mixer, lightly whisk together, without over-whisking. Add the lemon zest and juice and coconut cream and lightly stir to combine. Leave to stand for 15 minutes to allow the flavours to infuse.

Strain the mixture through a sieve into a large jug. Place the pastry case on the baking sheet in the oven. Pull the oven shelf out just enough to allow you to very gently pour the filling into the pastry case; it will be very full, so a steady hand is required.

Bake for 55–60 minutes or until the tart is firm but slightly wobbly in the middle. Set aside to cool.

To serve, sift icing sugar generously over the tart. If you have a cook's blowtorch, carefully run it over the surface to caramelise the crust. Alternatively, place the tart under a hot grill to caramelise, keeping a close eye on it as it can quickly burn.

RICH CHOCOLATE AND HAZELNUT TART

This is a very sophisticated and grown-up dessert, and oh-so-delicious. The first time I baked it my husband said, 'Just a very small slice please', closely followed by, 'Can I have another piece please?'. If you have any left over, which is highly unlikely, carefully wrap it in baking parchment and store in an airtight tin; don't put it in the fridge, or the pastry will quickly lose its crispness.

Serves: 8–10
Equipment: 23cm loose-bottomed tart tin; food processor (optional)
Preparation: 45 minutes plus minimum 1½ hours chilling, then cooling
Cooking time: Approx. 1 hour
Freeze: No

---

1 quantity Hazelnut Pastry (page 17)
1 egg, beaten with 1 tbsp soya, rice, almond or coconut milk

Chocolate Filling
200g blanched hazelnuts
400g best-quality (60% cocoa) dark, dairy-free chocolate, chopped
150ml soya, rice, almond or coconut milk
250ml single soya cream
2 large eggs, beaten

Make the pastry, wrap in clingfilm and chill in the fridge for at least 1 hour, or overnight if possible.

Preheat the oven to 190°C/ 170°C fan/Gas 5. Spread the hazelnuts out on a baking sheet and toast in the oven for 6–8 minutes or until they start to colour. Remove from the oven, tip onto a board and leave to cool for 5 minutes before roughly chopping. Clean the baking sheet and return it to the oven.

Roll out the chilled pastry to a rough circle slightly larger than the tart tin and 3mm thick (see page 14). Lightly prick the base with a fork and chill in the freezer for 30 minutes.

Line the pastry case with baking parchment and ceramic beans, place on the hot baking sheet in the oven and bake for 15 minutes or until the pastry starts to turn golden. Remove from the oven and lift the parchment and ceramic beans out; take care, as they will be very hot.

Brush the beaten egg and milk mixture over the pastry case. Return to the oven for 10 minutes or until the pastry is golden all over. Set aside to cool, and reduce the oven temperature to 150°C/130°C fan/Gas 2.

Put the chocolate into a large heatproof bowl. Bring the milk and cream to the boil in a heavy-based saucepan, pour over the chocolate and whisk until smooth. Add the beaten eggs and whisk again.

Pour the chocolate mixture into the cooled pastry case and scatter the chopped hazelnuts over the top, pressing them down lightly into the chocolate mixture.

Bake in the oven for 30–35 minutes until the mixture has started to set but still has a slight wobble in the middle. Leave to cool completely before serving.

BLUEBERRY AND RASPBERRY AMANDINES

The classic French Amandine is in fact like our own Bakewell tart; full of frangipane, or almond cream, and topped with flaked almonds, but without the layer of jam. Fresh berries provide a wonderfully tart foil to the sweetness of the almond cream and the juice from the cooked berries seeps through to add a richness of colour. Frangipane tarts freeze beautifully, with the pastry crisping up nicely when reheated.

Serves: 6
Equipment: Six 10cm shallow tartlet tins; food processor (optional)
Preparation time: 1 hour plus minimum 1½ hours chilling
Cooking time: Approx. 1 hour
Freeze: Yes – defrost fully and reheat in an oven preheated to 180°C/160°C fan/Gas 4 for 5–6 minutes

1 quantity Pâte Sucrée (page 18)
1 egg, beaten with 1 tbsp soya, rice, almond or coconut milk
220g mixture of blueberries and raspberries
30g flaked almonds
175g apricot jam
Juice of ¼ lemon
A little cold water

Frangipane Filling
100g dairy-free spread
100g unrefined caster sugar
1 large egg plus 1 large yolk, beaten
110g ground almonds
25g wheat- and gluten-free plain flour
2 tbsp Kirsch, crème de cassis or crème de framboise

Make the pastry and use to line the 6 tartlet tins (see page 14) and transfer to the freezer to chill for 30 minutes. Meanwhile, preheat the oven to 190°C/170°C fan/Gas 5 and place a baking sheet in the oven to heat. Line the chilled pastry cases with baking parchment and ceramic beans and transfer to the hot baking sheet in the oven. Blind bake for 15 minutes.

Remove from the oven and lift the parchment and beans out; take care, as they will be very hot. Brush the beaten egg and milk mixture over the pastry cases and return to the oven for 5–10 minutes. Set aside to cool and increase the oven temperature to 200°C/180°C fan/Gas 6.

For the filling, in a large bowl, beat the dairy-free spread and sugar together until light and creamy in colour. Gradually add the beaten egg and yolk, beating well after each addition.

Using a large metal spoon, gently stir in the ground almonds and flour, then stir in the liqueur. Pour the mixture into the tartlet cases, gently spreading it to the edges if necessary, using a round-bladed knife.

Gently press the berries into the filling, without cramming in too many. Sprinkle with the flaked almonds and bake in the oven for 10–15 minutes or until the pastry starts to brown.

Turn the oven down to 180°C/160°C fan/Gas 4 and continue baking for 15–20 minutes until the filling is firm to the touch.

Meanwhile, melt the apricot jam with the lemon juice and water in a small pan. Press through a nylon sieve into a small glass bowl.

Remove the tartlets from the oven and, using a pastry brush, generously paint the tops with the apricot glaze. Serve warm or cold with Coconut Cream or a scoop of Madagascan Vanilla Ice Cream.

TIP *The apricot glaze gives these tartlets a really professional finish and can also be used on fruit tarts large and small to give them that French polish and sheen. Don't let the jam boil or it will become sticky and glue-like, and if it starts to cool and thicken whilst you are painting your tarts, just gently reheat it until it becomes nice and fluid again.*

NUTMEG AND VANILLA CUSTARD TARTS WITH STRAWBERRY AND BALSAMIC COMPOTE

The heady sweetness of the vanilla and nutmeg in these little tarts makes them totally irresistible. You could serve these with a compote of any soft fruit, but not too much or you will drown out the beautiful flavour of the tarts.

Serves: 8
Equipment: Eight 9 x 3cm rectangular tartlet tins; food processor (optional); electric hand mixer
Preparation time: 1 hour plus 1½ hours chilling
Cooking time: Approx. 45 minutes
Freeze: No

1 quantity Pâte Sucrée (page 18)
1 egg, beaten with 1 tbsp soya, rice or almond milk

Custard Filling
600ml coconut milk
1 vanilla pod, split lengthways
6 large egg yolks
75g unrefined caster sugar
A grating of nutmeg

Strawberry Compote
400g strawberries, hulled
3 tbsp unrefined caster sugar
1½ tbsp lemon juice
¼ tsp balsamic vinegar (optional)

Make the pastry and use to line the 8 tartlet tins (see page 14), then blind bake in an oven preheated to 190°C/170°C fan/Gas 5, following the method on page 28 and brushing the pastry with the beaten egg and milk mixture for the last 5–10 minutes of baking. Set aside to cool.

For the filling, put the coconut milk in a small pan, scrape the seeds from the vanilla pod and add both the seeds and the pod to the milk. Gently heat to lukewarm.

Put the egg yolks and sugar into a mixing bowl and, using an electric hand mixer, beat until smooth and creamy.

Pour the warmed milk onto the yolk mixture and stir with a large wooden spoon until combined; don't whisk, as you don't want bubbles.

Strain the custard through a nylon sieve into a large jug and then carefully pour into the pastry cases. Sprinkle with grated nutmeg.

Bake in the oven for 20 minutes or until the custard is just wobbly. Leave to cool slightly before removing from their tins to a wire rack to cool completely.

To make the strawberry compote, cut the strawberries in half, or quarters if large. Place in a medium saucepan, add the sugar and lemon juice and slowly bring to the boil. Reduce the heat and simmer for about 5 minutes or until the strawberries have darkened in colour and the liquid has become thick and syrupy. Remove from the heat and leave to cool, then gently stir in the balsamic vinegar, if using.

Serve the little tarts with the cold strawberry compote.

TIP *If you don't have a vanilla pod to hand but have 3 fresh or dried bay leaves, add them to the milk to infuse the custard with their subtle flavour.*

FRENCH APRICOT TART

A simply stunning French classic that is always a huge hit with my husband. As much as I would love to use beautifully ripe apricots in this recipe, it isn't always possible. Even in summer I can struggle to find soft, juicy fruit with that distinctive heady aroma, so I don't hesitate to use tinned apricots instead. Once they have caramelised, it is difficult to tell the difference.

Serves: 10–12 **Equipment:** 25cm tart tin; food processor (optional) **Preparation time:** 1 hour plus minimum 1½ hours chilling **Cooking time:** Approx. 1 hour **Freeze:** No

---

1 quantity Pâte Sucrée (page 18)
1 egg, beaten with 1 tbsp soya, rice, almond or coconut milk

Filling
½ quantity Crème Pâtissière (page 146)
1 quantity Frangipane (page 150)
14 fresh apricots, quartered and stoned; or 2 cans apricot halves in syrup, drained and cut into quarters
2 tsp unrefined granulated sugar

Glaze
100g apricot jam
1 tbsp water

Make the pastry, wrap in clingfilm and chill in the fridge for at least 1 hour, or overnight if possible.

Roll out the chilled pastry to a rough circle slightly larger than the tart tin and 3mm thick (see page 14). Use to line the tin, then lightly prick the base with a fork and chill in the freezer for 30 minutes. Meanwhile, preheat the oven to 190°C/170°C fan/Gas 5 and place a baking sheet in the oven to heat.

Line the pastry case with baking parchment and ceramic beans. Place in the oven on the hot baking sheet and bake for 15 minutes or until the pastry is starting to turn golden. Remove from the oven and lift the parchment and ceramic beans out; take care, as they will be very hot.

Brush the pastry case with the beaten egg and milk mixture and return to the oven for 10 minutes or until the pastry is golden. Set aside to cool, and reduce the oven temperature to 180°C/160°C fan/Gas 4.

Combine the Crème Pâtissière and the Frangipane in a bowl, mix well and use to fill the cooled pastry case.

Place the quartered fresh or canned apricots on top of the frangipane, skin side down, pressing gently into the frangipane so that one end of each quarter sticks up slightly.

Sprinkle the apricots with the sugar and bake in the oven for 35–40 minutes. The pastry should be a nice dark brown and the apricot tips will have caramelised.

Leave to cool for 20 minutes, then remove the tart from the tin and place on a cooling rack.

Gently warm the apricot jam and water in a small saucepan until it starts to simmer; don't let it boil. Remove from the heat and, using a pastry brush, lightly paint the apricots.

RASPBERRY CREME PATISSIERE TARTLETS

I love making these beautiful little French tartlets when I want to impress my friends. They look a million dollars but are deceptively easy and quick to make, especially if you make the pastry and crème pâtissière the day before and refrigerate them overnight.

Serves: 8
Equipment: Eight rectangular 11 x 6cm loose-bottomed tartlet tins (or one round 23cm tart tin); food processor (optional); electric hand mixer; piping bag fitted with a nozzle (optional)
Preparation time: 1 hour plus minimum 1½ hours chilling
Cooking time: 15–20 minutes
Freeze: No

Pastry
½ quantity Sweet Shortcrust Pastry (page 16)
50g white chocolate couverture powder

Filling
1 quantity Crème Pâtissière (page 146), chilled
350g raspberries
4 tbsp redcurrant jelly
Juice of ¼ lemon
2 tbsp cold water

TIP *Any leftover glaze can be stored in a sterilised jam jar in the fridge for future use.*

Make the pastry, wrap in clingfilm and chill in the fridge for a minimum of 1 hour, or overnight if possible.

Divide the chilled pastry roughly into 8 pieces. Keep one piece and return the others, wrapped, to the fridge.

Place the pastry piece on a small sheet of clingfilm lightly dusted with flour. Place another small sheet of clingfilm over the top of the pastry and gently start to roll it out into a rough circle 3mm thick. You might need to pull the clingfilm taut after several rolls to ensure it doesn't get caught in the pastry. Remove the top sheet of clingfilm, then lift the bottom sheet up and turn over onto a tartlet tin. Gently press the pastry into place before peeling the clingfilm off. Trim the excess pastry by rolling the rolling pin across the top of the tin. Lightly prick the base with a fork. Repeat for the remaining 7 tart tins.

Place the tart tins in the freezer to chill for 30 minutes. Preheat the oven to 190°C/170°C fan/Gas 5 and put in a baking sheet to heat.

Line the chilled pastry cases with baking parchment and baking beans. Blind bake on the hot baking sheet for 10–15 minutes or until the pastry starts to turn golden.

Remove the pastry cases from the oven and lift the parchment and beans out; be careful, as they will be very hot. Return the pastry cases to the oven for a further 5 minutes or until the bases are also golden. Remove from the oven and leave to cool.

Melt the white chocolate couverture powder in a glass mixing bowl over a saucepan of barely simmering water, making sure the base of the bowl doesn't touch the water otherwise the chocolate will seize.

Spoon 2 teaspoons of the melted chocolate into each cold pastry case. Using a pastry brush, paint up the sides and across the base of the cases. Leave to cool for 30 minutes, then chill in the fridge until cold.

Give the chilled Crème Pâtissière a quick whisk to loosen it, then spoon or pipe it into the chilled pastry cases. Cover with the raspberries.

Put the redcurrant jelly, lemon juice and water into a small saucepan and gently heat until the jam has dissolved. Using the pastry brush, carefully paint the glaze over the raspberries. Eat on the same day.

LEMON MERINGUE PIE

Whilst lemon meringue pies were always a huge hit with my friends at school, I'm embarrassed to admit I preferred cocoa pop cake with pink custard! Anyway, 40 years later it would appear nothing much has changed in our schools, as according to my son Charlie, lemon meringue pie is still a firm favourite with all his friends. I like my lemon curd filling really tart, but if you prefer it on the sweeter side, just add a little more caster sugar when bringing the curd to the boil.

Serves: 6–8
Equipment: 20cm, deep tart tin; food processor (optional); electric hand mixer
Preparation time: 30 minutes plus minimum 1½ hours chilling
Cooking time: Approx. 50 minutes
Freeze: No

½ quantity Sweet Shortcrust Pastry (page 16)
1 egg, beaten with 1 tbsp soya, rice, almond or coconut milk

Lemon Filling
200ml lemon juice (approx. 5 lemons)
50ml orange juice (1–2 oranges)
150g unrefined caster sugar
25g cornflour
3 large eggs, separated
25g dairy-free spread

Meringue
4 large egg whites (3 reserved from the filling, plus 1 extra)
115g unrefined caster sugar
115g icing sugar

Make the pastry, wrap in clingfilm and chill in the fridge for at least 1 hour, or overnight if possible.

Roll out the chilled pastry to a rough circle slightly larger than the tart tin and 3mm thick (see page 14). Use to line the tin, then lightly prick the base with a fork and chill in the freezer for 30 minutes. Meanwhile, preheat the oven to 190°C/170°C fan/Gas 5 and place a baking sheet in the oven to heat.

Line the pastry case with baking parchment and ceramic beans. Place in the oven on the hot baking sheet and bake for 15 minutes or until the pastry is starting to turn golden. Remove from the oven and lift the parchment and ceramic beans out; take care, as they will be very hot.

Brush the pastry case with the beaten egg and milk mixture and return to the oven for 10 minutes or until the pastry is golden all over. Set aside to cool, and reduce the oven temperature to 170°C/150°C fan/Gas 3.

For the filling, put the lemon and orange juice into a medium saucepan with the sugar, cornflour and egg yolks. Whisk over a medium heat until smooth, then add the dairy-free spread and whisk to combine. Whisking constantly, bring to the boil, then pour the mixture into the pastry case and leave to cool completely.

To make the meringue, put the egg whites in a big glass or metal bowl. Whisk to stiff peaks with an electric hand mixer on medium speed.

Increase the speed and gradually add the caster sugar 1 tablespoon at a time, beating for a few seconds between each addition, until it is all incorporated and the whites are thick and glossy. Sift one third of the icing sugar into the whites and fold in using a large metal spoon. Repeat twice more, but don't over-mix.

It's really important that the lemon curd filling is cold at this stage; if it's still warm, the meringue you put on top will start to leak syrup. Pile the meringue onto the cold lemon curd, make decorative peaks and bake the tart in the oven for 25–30 minutes or until lovely and golden. Leave to cool before serving.

TARTE TOUT CHOCOLAT

Wow: if you love chocolate, then this is the tart for you. It is incredibly rich, starting soft and gooey in the centre before firming up into a rich and decadent mousse the longer it is left to cool. The added layer of sweetly sour Blackcurrant Ripple makes it spectacularly delicious.

Serves: 8–10
Equipment: 25cm loose-bottomed, deep tart tin; food processor (optional); electric hand mixer
Preparation time: 1 hour plus minimum 1½ hours chilling
Cooking time: Approx. 50 minutes
Freeze: No

---

1 quantity Chocolate Pâte Sucrée (page 19)
60g best-quality (60% cocoa) dark, dairy-free chocolate, chopped

Filling
400g best-quality (60% cocoa) dark, dairy-free chocolate, chopped
125g dairy-free spread
5 large eggs, separated
125g unrefined caster sugar
150ml double rice cream
2 tbsp dark rum
200g Blackcurrant Ripple (page 142) or good-quality conserve

TIP *I use a double rice cream here, but if you can't find it you can substitute it with single soya cream or a rich coconut cream; the tart will taste just as fantastic.*

Make the pastry, wrap in clingfilm and chill in the fridge for at least 1 hour, or overnight if possible.

Roll out the chilled pastry to a rough circle slightly larger than the tart tin and 3mm thick (see page 14). Use to line the tin, lightly prick the base with a fork and chill in the freezer for 30 minutes. Meanwhile, preheat the oven to 190°C/170°C fan/Gas 5 and place a baking sheet in the oven to heat.

Line the pastry case with baking parchment and ceramic beans, place on the hot baking sheet in the oven and bake for 15 minutes. Remove from the oven and lift the parchment and ceramic beans out; take care, as they will be very hot. Bake for a further 10 minutes, then set aside to cool. Reduce the oven temperature to 180°C/160°C fan/Gas 4.

Melt the 60g chocolate in a heatproof bowl set over a saucepan of barely simmering water, making sure the base of the bowl isn't touching the water.

Spoon the melted chocolate into the cold pastry case and, using a pastry brush, gently paint up the sides and across the base of the case. Leave to cool for 10 minutes, then chill in the fridge to harden while you make the filling.

Melt the 400g chocolate with the dairy-free spread in a heatproof bowl set over a saucepan of barely simmering water.

Put the egg yolks and caster sugar into a bowl and, using an electric hand mixer, whisk until light and creamy.

Stir the cream and rum into the melted chocolate, then quickly fold in the egg yolk and sugar mixture.

In a clean bowl, whisk the egg whites to soft peaks, then carefully fold into the chocolate mixture.

Spread the Blackcurrant Ripple or conserve evenly in the cold pastry case, then pour in the chocolate mixture to come all the way to the top. Bake for 25–30 minutes. The filling will puff up, but the surface should be firm to the touch with a gentle wobble in the centre.

Leave to cool completely, as the filling will firm and crack as it cools. Serve with a swirl of coconut cream.

BUTTERSCOTCH MERINGUE TARTLETS

Toffee, caramel and butterscotch have always been a favourite of mine, so filling a crisp pastry case with a rich butterscotch custard and topping it with crunchy meringue peaks is a bit of a no-brainer for me. These tartlets are best eaten slightly warm on the day they are made, with a scoop of vanilla ice cream or just on their own.

Serves: 6
Equipment: Six 9 x 3cm tartlet tins; food processor (optional); electric hand mixer; piping bag fitted with an 806 stainless steel nozzle (optional)
Preparation time: 1 hour plus minimum 1½ hours chilling
Cooking time: Approx. 1 hour
Freeze: No

1 quantity Pâte Sucrée (page 18)
1 egg, beaten with 1 tbsp soya, rice, almond or coconut milk

Butterscotch Filling

4 large egg yolks
3 tbsp cornflour
300ml soya, rice, almond or coconut milk
85g dairy-free spread
175g light muscovado sugar
1 tsp vanilla extract

Meringue Topping

4 large egg whites
120g unrefined caster sugar
120g icing sugar

TIP *I like my meringue tips lightly browned, and the best way to do this is with a cook's blowtorch. If you don't have one, pop the tartlets under a hot grill for a few minutes.*

Make the pastry and use to line the 6 tartlet tins (see page 14), then blind bake in an oven preheated to 190°C/170°C fan/Gas 5, following the method on page 28 and brushing the pastry with the beaten egg and milk mixture for the last 5–10 minutes of baking. Set aside to cool and reduce the oven temperature to 150°C/130°C fan/Gas 2.

For the filling, put the egg yolks in a medium bowl and, in a small bowl, mix the cornflour to a paste with a little of the milk.

Gently melt the dairy-free spread in a medium, heavy-based saucepan, add the sugar and stir until dissolved.

Add the remaining milk with the cornflour paste and slowly bring to the boil, stirring constantly to prevent sticking. Simmer for a couple of minutes so that the mixture starts to thicken, then set aside off the heat for 5 minutes to cool slightly.

Pour about a third of the cooled mixture onto the egg yolks, whisking continuously to prevent lumps, then return to the pan with the rest of the milk mixture. Stirring constantly, bring to the boil and simmer for a couple of minutes until thick. Remove from the heat and beat in the vanilla extract.

To make the meringue, whisk the egg whites to stiff peaks in a very clean metal or glass bowl, using an electric hand mixer on a medium speed. Increase the speed and add the caster sugar, a dessertspoonful at a time, whisking between additions.

Sift a third of the icing sugar into the bowl and fold in using a large metal spoon. Repeat until all the icing sugar has been incorporated and the meringue is firm and glossy.

Spoon the butterscotch custard into the cooled pastry cases.

Place the meringue mixture in the piping bag and gently pipe the mixture in small swirls over the top of the still warm butterscotch. If you don't have a piping bag, just spoon on the meringue, using the back of the spoon to make the swirls.

Return the tartlets to the oven for 30–35 minutes, then leave to cool to just warm before serving.

CARAMELISED BANANA PIE

I can still vividly remember making my first upside-down pudding at school age 14, using pineapple slices and glacé cherries. My teacher, Miss Stevens, was a bit of a spoilsport and we weren't allowed to eat it, so I carefully carried it all the way home where I dutifully served it to my family – cold! I'm sure the caramelised pineapple was delicious, but I like to think my baking skills have come a long way since then, and whilst the principle of turning the pudding upside down has remained the same, I'm happy to report the quality of the finished pie has improved considerably.

Serves: 8–10
Equipment: 25cm heavy-based, ovenproof frying pan or specialist Tarte Tatin pan; electric hand mixer
Preparation time: 30 minutes
Cooking time: Approx. 45–50 minutes
Freeze: No

Base

75g dairy-free spread
45g coconut palm sugar or unrefined soft light brown sugar
45g unrefined caster sugar
3 large bananas
A squeeze of lemon juice

Topping

1 ripe banana, mashed
2 tbsp coconut cream
1 tsp vanilla extract
75g dairy-free spread
150g unrefined caster sugar
2 large eggs, beaten
175g wheat- and gluten-free self-raising flour
1 tsp xanthan gum

Preheat the oven to 180°C/160°C fan/Gas 4.

Melt the dairy-free spread in the ovenproof frying or Tarte Tatin pan over a low heat. Add both sugars and stir to dissolve. Once they have dissolved, remove the pan from the heat.

Cut the bananas into slices the thickness of a £1 coin and carefully arrange in concentric circles over the base of the pan. Squeeze a little lemon juice over the bananas to keep them from going brown.

To make the topping, mix the mashed banana with the coconut cream and vanilla extract in a bowl.

In a separate bowl, using an electric hand mixer, cream the dairy-free spread and sugar together until nice and fluffy.

Gradually add the beaten eggs and beat until combined.

Sift the flour and xanthan gum together, then carefully fold into the egg mixture, alternating twice with the banana and coconut cream mixture until everything is combined.

Carefully dot the mixture over the bananas in the pan, then smooth it over the bananas using a round-bladed or palette knife. Don't worry if it looks as though you don't have enough topping; the thin layer will rise as it cooks.

Bake in the oven for 45–50 minutes or until golden brown and firm to the touch.

Rest the pie for 10 minutes before very carefully inverting onto a serving plate, so that the caramelised banana is on top.

Serve warm with softly whipped coconut cream or your favourite ice cream.

PROPER APPLE PIE

Everyone I know loves apple pie, so they certainly don't need to be reminded of its merits. For good measure, though, this apple pie is seriously good and everyone should make it!

Serves: 6–8 **Equipment:** 20cm springform cake tin; food processor (optional) **Preparation time:** 1 hour plus minimum 1½ hours chilling **Cooking time:** 45–50 minutes **Freeze:** No

---

1 quantity Sweet Shortcrust Pastry (page 16)
1 egg, beaten with 1 tbsp soya, rice, almond or coconut milk
Unrefined granulated sugar, to sprinkle

Filling
750g Bramley apples
750g Cox's apples, peeled, cored and chopped into 1cm chunks
1 tbsp dairy-free spread
1 cinnamon stick
6 cloves
100g light muscovado sugar
1 tbsp wheat- and gluten-free plain flour
1 tbsp unrefined demerara sugar
Juice of ½ lemon

Apple Sauce Liquor
Peel and cores from the Bramley apples
500ml apple juice
100g unrefined caster sugar

Make the pastry, wrap in clingfilm and chill in the fridge for at least 1 hour, or overnight if possible.

Divide the chilled pastry into two pieces – three quarters and one quarter. Wrap and chill the small piece, and roll out the larger piece to a circle 5mm thick (see page 14). Use to line the springform tin, then lightly prick the base with a fork and chill in the freezer for 30 minutes. Meanwhile, preheat the oven to 190°C/170°C fan/Gas 5.

Blind bake the pastry case following the method on page 32. Reserve the remaining beaten egg and milk mixture for the pie top, later.

Meanwhile, peel, core and chop the Bramley apples into 1cm chunks. For the apple sauce liquor, put the peel and cores in a saucepan, add the apple juice and sugar and simmer for 20 minutes. Remove from the heat, strain and return to the pan to reduce for 10 minutes.

Put the dairy-free spread into a large saucepan, add the cinnamon and cloves and gently melt the spread over a low heat. Add the muscovado sugar and stir to mix. Add the chopped Bramley apples and cook for a few minutes over a high heat until the juices start to run, then cover, reduce the heat and cook for 10–15 minutes. Remove the cinnamon stick and stir the apples vigorously a couple of times until they disintegrate into a purée. Remove from the heat and leave to cool.

Sprinkle the base of the pastry case with the flour and demerara sugar.

Stir the lemon juice and 50ml of the apple sauce liquor (reserve the rest) into the Bramley purée before adding the chopped Cox's. Pour the apple mixture into the pastry case.

Roll out the remaining pastry and cut out 8 or 10 strips, 2.5cm wide. Place across the top of the pie in an interwoven criss-cross pattern. Pinch the strips to the edge of the pastry case. Brush the pastry with the beaten egg and milk mixture, then sprinkle with granulated sugar.

Bake in the oven for 45–50 minutes or until the top is crisp and golden brown. Leave to cool for 10 minutes before releasing from the tin. Serve warm with Walnut Praline Ice Cream and the apple sauce liquor.

HERE ARE THE
UNASHAMEDLY
NOSTALGIC AND
GLORIOUS PUDDINGS
OF MY CHILDHOOD:
STICKY TOFFEE
PUDDING, JAM
ROLY-POLY, STEAMED
GINGER SPONGE,
RHUBARB CRUMBLE...

Traditional Puddings

CHARLIE'S PECAN STICKY TOFFEE PUDDINGS

This is my son Charlie's all-time favourite pudding, and quite possibly mine as well, so at his request I have named it in his honour. Enjoy.

Serves: 8
Equipment: Eight 180ml pudding basins or dariole moulds; electric hand mixer
Preparation time: 1 hour
Cooking time: Approx. 30 minutes
Freeze: Yes – wrap the cooled puddings individually in clingfilm and freeze for up to 3 months. Defrost at room temperature before reheating in the sauce

225g dates (ideally Medjool)
175ml boiling water
1 tsp vanilla extract
85g dairy-free spread, plus extra for greasing
140g unrefined soft light brown sugar
2 large eggs, beaten
2 tbsp black treacle
175g wheat- and gluten-free self-raising flour, plus extra for dusting
1 tsp xanthan gum
1 tsp bicarbonate of soda
100ml soya, rice, almond or coconut milk

Sticky Toffee Sauce
50g dairy-free spread
175g light muscovado sugar
225ml soya, rice, almond or oat cream
1 tbsp black treacle
25g pecan nuts, chopped

Stone the dates, then chop them quite finely and place in a heatproof bowl before covering with the boiling water. Add the vanilla extract and leave to soak for 30 minutes.

Meanwhile, grease and lightly flour the basins or darioles and place on a baking sheet. Preheat the oven to 180°C/160°C fan/Gas 4.

Using an electric hand mixer, beat the dairy-free spread and sugar together in a large mixing bowl, then gradually add the beaten eggs a little at a time; don't worry if the mixture looks a little curdled. Add the black treacle and beat to combine.

Sift the flour, xanthan gum and bicarbonate of soda together. Using a large metal spoon, carefully and lightly fold one third into the egg mixture, then fold in half the milk. Repeat until all the flour and milk has been incorporated, but don't over-stir.

Add the dates and their soaking water and stir to combine into a thick, sloppy batter.

Divide the mixture evenly between the basins or darioles and bake in the oven for 20–25 minutes until nicely risen and firm to the touch. Set aside to cool for 5 minutes.

For the sauce, bring the dairy-free spread, sugar and half the cream gently to the boil in a small, heavy-based saucepan, stirring all the time. Stir in the black treacle, then increase the heat and allow the sauce to bubble for 2–3 minutes, stirring occasionally to make sure the sugar doesn't burn.

Remove from the heat and stir in the remaining cream. Pour half the sauce into an ovenproof serving dish.

Using a cloth to protect your hands, slide a small palette knife around the sides of each basin or dariole, then carefully turn the puddings out into the serving dish.

Add the chopped pecans to the remaining sauce and drizzle over the top of the puddings. Cover the dish with a tent of foil and place back in the oven for 5 minutes.

Serve the puddings hot with Madagascan Vanilla Ice Cream or whipped Coconut Cream.

MY MUM'S CHRISTMAS PUDDING

For some reason, family traditions become more important to us at Christmas and in our house it's the foodie ones that matter most. The centrepiece of our festive dinner is the wonderfully moist Christmas pud. With the lights turned down low and the air full of flaming brandy fumes, it is carried with great ceremony to the table where its beauty of form is much admired.

Serves: 8 **Equipment:** 1.5 litre pudding basin; very large saucepan (to fit basin) or casserole dish with a lid
Preparation time: 45 minutes plus overnight marinating **Cooking time:** 8 hours **Freeze:** No need; once cooked, store in a dry, cool cupboard

90g sultanas
90g currants
90g raisins
90g dates, stoned and chopped
90g dried cranberries
2 tbsp thick-cut marmalade, peel roughly chopped
1 small cooking apple, peeled, cored and finely chopped
Grated zest and juice of ½ orange
Grated zest and juice of ½ lemon
4 tbsp brandy, plus extra to drizzle
55g wheat- and gluten-free self-raising flour
½ tsp xanthan gum
1½ tsp ground cinnamon
1 tsp ground mixed spice
110g wheat- and gluten-free vegetarian suet
110g unrefined soft dark brown sugar
110g white wheat- and gluten-free breadcrumbs
25g almonds, roughly chopped
2 large eggs, lightly beaten
Dairy-free spread, for greasing

Put the dried fruit, marmalade, apple, orange and lemon juice and zest into a large mixing bowl, add the brandy and stir really well. Cover and leave to marinate overnight.

Next day, mix the flour, xanthan gum, cinnamon and mixed spice together in another large mixing bowl. Add the suet, sugar, breadcrumbs and almonds and stir really well to combine, then add the soaked fruit and stir again. Stir in the beaten eggs; the mixture should now be nice and soft. It was at this point that my younger sister and I took turns in having a really good stir; we made lots of wishes and dropped in lots of sixpences, which rather shows my age!

Lightly grease the pudding basin before spooning the mixture in, gently pressing down with the back of the spoon. Cover the pudding basin with 2 layers of baking parchment and a layer of baking foil, each with a 2.5cm pleat to allow the pudding room to expand. Tie tightly with string around the rim.

Put an upturned saucer in the base of a large saucepan that will fit the pudding, and place the pudding basin on top. Half-fill the pan with boiling water and place the lid on tightly (this is important). Steam the pudding in simmering water for 7 hours, checking the level of the water frequently so that it doesn't boil dry.

Take the pan off the heat, carefully remove the pudding from the pan and leave to cool completely.

Remove the foil and baking parchment, prick the surface of the pudding with a skewer and drizzle over a little brandy. Cover with new baking parchment and foil and secure with string. Store in a cool, dry place until Christmas Day.

To reheat, steam the pudding again for 1 hour. Serve with either warm custard, vanilla ice cream, coconut cream or all three!

INDIVIDUAL RHUBARB, ORANGE AND HAZELNUT CRUMBLES

I have suggested using forced rhubarb in this recipe for a number of reasons: firstly, because it appears in the shops in early February; secondly, it has a more delicate flavour than later maincrop rhubarb; and lastly, because it has a beautiful pink colour that in the depths of winter offers a hope of better times to come. You can of course use maincrop rhubarb, but you might find that you need to peel the tough, stringy skin before chopping into bite-sized pieces.

Serves: 6
Equipment: Six 180ml ramekins; food processor (optional)
Preparation time: 20 minutes
Cooking time: Approx. 40 minutes
Freeze: Yes – cool the crumble to room temperature. Cover each with clingfilm and foil and freeze for up to 3 months. Defrost overnight in the fridge, remove the clingfilm, cover with foil and reheat for 25 minutes at 190°C/170°C fan/Gas 5

500g trimmed forced rhubarb
Grated zest of 1 large orange
6 tsp unrefined caster sugar
2 tsp cornflour

Crumble Topping

35g blanched hazelnuts
110g wheat- and gluten-free
  plain flour
½ tsp xanthan gum
75g dairy-free block margarine or
  solid coconut oil, cubed
35g unrefined demerara sugar
40g unrefined caster sugar

Preheat the oven to 180°C/160°C fan/Gas 4.

Spread the hazelnuts for the topping on a baking tray and toast in the oven for 6–8 minutes or until golden brown. Tip onto a plate to cool.

Wash and thoroughly dry the rhubarb, then chop into 2.5cm pieces.

Place in a large bowl with the orange zest, then rub it in using your fingers so that each piece of rhubarb is coated in zest.

Divide the rhubarb evenly between the 6 ramekins, packing it all in so that the crumble mixture doesn't drop down between the pieces during cooking.

Put the 6 teaspoons caster sugar into a small bowl with the cornflour, mix well to combine completely, then sprinkle evenly over the rhubarb.

To make the topping, if using a food processor, put the flour, xanthan gum and block margarine or coconut oil cubes into the bowl and pulse gently until it resembles coarse breadcrumbs; a few larger lumps will just add nicely to the crumble texture. Alternatively, put the ingredients into a large mixing bowl and rub in using your fingertips.

Roughly chop the toasted hazelnuts and add with the demerara and 40g caster sugar to the crumble mixture.

Sprinkle the crumble mixture over the rhubarb and bake in the oven for 30–35 minutes or until golden brown and bubbling.

Remove from the oven and leave to cool for 30 minutes. Crumble tastes much better when it is warm rather than hot, and cold crumble with warm vanilla custard is just heavenly. Alternatively, serve with vanilla ice cream.

TIP *Although I have flavoured the rhubarb with orange here, it also works well with ginger. Chop 2 pieces of stem ginger in syrup into small pieces and add to the ramekins; if you like a really strong ginger flavour, add a teaspoon of the syrup as well, but don't be tempted to add more or the liquid will overpower the crumble as it cooks.*

STEAMED GINGER SPONGES

On a cold winter's day, with a gale blowing and the rain pouring down, I love nothing better than serving this warming pudding with a steaming jug of delicious custard or a dollop of cold vanilla ice cream – heavenly. To make one large pudding, use a 1.5 litre basin and steam for 2 hours.

Serves: 6
Equipment: Six 180ml pudding basins or dariole moulds; food processor
Preparation time: 20 minutes
Cooking time: 1½ hours
Freeze: Yes – either uncooked or cooked. Wrap well in foil in their basins or darioles and freeze for up to 3 months. If cooked, steam for 45 minutes–1 hour to defrost and heat through. If uncooked, follow the instructions for steaming and add an extra 30 minutes for defrosting

Vegetable oil, for greasing
100g wheat- and gluten-free self-raising flour
1 tsp xanthan gum
1 heaped tsp bicarbonate of soda
2 heaped tsp ground ginger
1 tsp ground mixed spice
100g wheat- and gluten-free white breadcrumbs
100g wheat- and gluten-free vegetarian suet
¼ tsp salt
150g stem ginger in syrup, plus 100ml of the syrup
200ml soya, rice, almond, oat or coconut milk
50g golden syrup, plus 4 tbsp
75g black treacle
1 large egg, beaten

Grease the pudding basins or dariole moulds with vegetable oil.

Half-fill a large saucepan or casserole with water and place an upturned saucer in the base. Start heating the water on a medium–high heat so it's ready to begin steaming the puddings straight away.

Sift the flour, xanthan gum, bicarbonate of soda, ground ginger and mixed spice into a large bowl. Mix in the breadcrumbs, suet and salt.

Set aside 4 tablespoons of stem ginger in syrup, and put the remainder with the ginger pieces into a food processor. Pulse until the ginger is coarsely chopped.

Gently heat the milk, half the chopped ginger, the 50g golden syrup and all the black treacle in a heavy-based saucepan, just to warm through; don't let it boil.

Add the liquid ingredients to the dry ingredients with the egg and beat with a wooden spoon until combined; it should be nice and sloppy.

Combine the 2 tablespoons golden syrup, 2 tablespoons reserved ginger syrup and the remaining chopped ginger in a small bowl, then divide evenly between the greased basins or darioles. Gently spoon the pudding mixture on top.

Cover each basin with baking parchment, greased with a little vegetable oil and pleated down the middle to allow room for the puddings to expand. Top each with foil and secure around the rim with string. Gently place in the saucepan on top of the upturned saucer and secure the lid. Steam for 1½ hours, adding more water to the pan if it looks like boiling dry.

Just before serving, gently heat the remaining 2 tablespoons each of golden and ginger syrup in a small, heavy-based saucepan, just to warm through; don't allow it to boil.

Take the saucepan off the heat and very carefully remove the basins. Leave to cool for 10 minutes, then take the foil and parchment off the basins and gently turn out onto serving dishes.

To serve, drizzle the warmed syrup lightly over the sponge and serve with custard or vanilla ice cream.

JENNY'S SYRUP SUET PUDDING

This is my late mother's much-loved and treasured recipe. I'm not sure where it originated from and unfortunately I never thought to ask, but over the years I have experimented with some of the ingredients – adding a little pinch of something here, removing a little bit of something there – but somehow the results have never tasted as good as hers. I always serve this with proper vanilla custard (page 139), which isn't too sweet, but my son Charlie assures me a good squirt of soya spray cream is just as good, if not better!

Serves: 4–6 **Equipment:** 1.5 litre pudding basin; very large saucepan or casserole dish (to fit basin)
Preparation time: 20 minutes **Cooking time:** 2 hours **Freeze:** Yes – either uncooked or cooked. Wrap well in foil in its basin and freeze for up to 3 months. If cooked, steam for 45 minutes–1 hour to defrost and heat through. If uncooked, follow the instructions for steaming and add an extra 30 minutes for defrosting

For the Basin
Dairy-free spread, for greasing
6 tbsp golden syrup
Juice of ¼ lemon

Pudding
100g wheat- and gluten-free
    self-raising flour
1 tsp xanthan gum
¼ tsp salt
1 rounded tsp bicarbonate of soda
100g wheat- and gluten-free
    vegetarian suet
100g wheat- and gluten-free white
    breadcrumbs
Grated zest of 1 orange
200ml soya, rice, almond or
    coconut milk
50g unrefined soft dark brown sugar
50g golden syrup
1 large egg, beaten

Half-fill the very large saucepan or casserole with water and place an upturned saucer in the base. Start heating the water over a medium to high heat.

Lightly grease the pudding basin with dairy-free spread.

Put the 6 tablespoons golden syrup and the lemon juice into the base of the pudding basin.

Sift the flour, xanthan gum, salt and bicarbonate of soda into a large mixing bowl. Add the suet, breadcrumbs and orange zest and mix well.

Put the milk, sugar and golden syrup into a medium saucepan and gently heat until the sugar has dissolved; do not let it boil.

Beat the warmed milk mixture into the dry ingredients and add the beaten egg. The mixture needs to be slightly sloppy.

Gently pour the mixture into the prepared basin, making sure the syrup and lemon juice mixture doesn't get pushed up the sides.

Cover the basin with baking parchment, greased with a little dairy-free spread and pleated down the middle to allow room for the pudding to expand. Top with foil and secure with string. Carefully place in the saucepan on top of the upturned saucer, and cover with the lid. Steam for 2 hours, checking the water occasionally so that it doesn't boil dry.

Take the pan off the heat and very carefully remove the basin. Leave to cool for 10 minutes, then remove the foil and baking parchment and gently turn out onto a serving dish.

Serve warm with Rich and Creamy Vanilla Custard, ice cream or soya spray cream!

ST STEPHEN'S PUDDING

I love all wintry suet puddings; they remind me of cold frosty mornings, steamy kitchens, Sunday lunches and the comfort of childhood. Although this particular pudding is often suggested as an alternative to Christmas pud, as children my sister and I would have happily eaten it every weekend. It's a surprisingly light but hearty pudding that is quick to prepare, and then just steams away in the background until needed.

Serves: 4–6 **Equipment:** Large saucepan or casserole dish; 1 litre pudding basin **Preparation time:** 20 minutes **Cooking time:** 2½ hours **Freeze:** Yes – either uncooked or cooked. Wrap well in foil in its basin and freeze for up to 3 months. If cooked, steam for 45 minutes–1 hour to defrost and heat through. If uncooked, follow the instructions for steaming and add an extra 30 minutes for defrosting

---

Dairy-free spread, for greasing
2 tbsp unrefined demerara sugar
110g wheat- and gluten-free white breadcrumbs
50g wheat- and gluten-free self-raising flour
½ tsp xanthan gum
½ tsp ground cinnamon
50g light muscovado sugar
75g wheat- and gluten-free vegetarian suet
¼ tsp salt
110g sultanas
200g Bramley apples
Grated zest and juice of 1 lemon
1 tbsp soya, rice, almond or coconut milk

Half-fill a large saucepan or casserole with water and place a saucer upside down in the base. Start heating the water over a medium to high heat.

Lightly grease the pudding basin with dairy-free spread and dust with the demerara sugar.

Put the breadcrumbs, flour, xanthan gum, cinnamon, muscovado sugar, suet, salt and sultanas into a large mixing bowl.

Peel the apples and coarsely grate into the bowl, sprinkling with the lemon zest and juice. Mix thoroughly, then stir in the milk. The mixture should have a soft, but not quite dropping, consistency.

Spoon the mixture into the prepared basin, firmly pushing it down so that there are no air pockets.

Cover the basin with baking parchment, lightly greased with dairy-free spread and pleated down the middle to allow room for the pudding to expand, top with foil and secure with string. Carefully place in the saucepan on top of the upturned saucer, and cover with the lid. Steam for 2½ hours, checking the water level occasionally so that it doesn't boil dry.

Take the saucepan off the heat and very carefully remove the basin. Leave to cool for 10 minutes, then remove the foil and baking parchment and gently turn out onto a serving dish.

Serve with custard or ice cream of your choice.

WARM AND GOOEY
CHOCOLATE FONDANT PUDDINGS

These wonderful little puddings never fail to amaze, and by popular demand feature regularly at my supper table. For puddings so delicious and impressive they are incredibly easy to make; just don't be tempted to leave them in the oven a minute longer than I tell you.

Serves: 6 **Equipment:** Six 180ml pudding basins or moulds; electric hand mixer **Preparation time:** 30 minutes **Cooking time:** 8–9 minutes **Freeze:** No

---

For the Moulds
Dairy-free spread, for greasing
2 tbsp cocoa powder

Fondant Puddings
125g best-quality (60% cocoa) dark, dairy-free chocolate, broken into pieces
125g dairy-free spread
4 large eggs
75g unrefined icing sugar, sifted
50g wheat- and gluten-free self-raising flour
35g cocoa powder

TIP *If you are serving these at a dinner party, they can happily be made the day before and chilled in the fridge overnight. Pop them into the oven just before serving.*

Preheat the oven to 180°C/160°C fan/Gas 4.

Grease the pudding basins or moulds with dairy-free spread and dust the insides with the cocoa powder.

Melt the chocolate and dairy-free spread in a heatproof bowl set over a pan of barely simmering water, making sure the base of the bowl doesn't touch the water or the chocolate will seize. Stir until combined, then remove the pan from the heat and the bowl from the pan. Set aside to cool a little.

Whisk the eggs and icing sugar together in a bowl with an electric hand mixer until light and foamy, 3–4 minutes.

Using a large metal spoon, gently fold the egg and sugar mixture into the cooled chocolate mixture, then sift in the flour and cocoa powder and carefully fold until combined.

Spoon the mixture evenly into the prepared basins and place them on a baking sheet. Bake for 8–9 minutes. They should rise nicely but have a soft and runny centre.

Using a flat-bladed knife, gently loosen each fondant from the sides of the basin, and carefully turn out each onto a serving plate.

Serve with Coffee Crème Anglaise for a wonderfully sophisticated dessert, or work the 1970s vibe and serve with Madagascan Vanilla Ice Cream and cherries soaked in Kirsch (found in good delis and at Christmas time in the major supermarkets).

GINGERBREAD SOUFFLÉS

If you have never made a soufflé before, then this warm and spicy, light and fluffy soufflé is the perfect place to start. The most important thing to remember is that they need to be made and baked just before eating; a soufflé will collapse within minutes of leaving the oven, and whilst it may taste divine, it is even nicer when it looks the part as well.

Serves: 8 **Equipment:** Eight 115ml ramekins; electric hand mixer **Preparation time:** 30 minutes
Cooking time: 10–11 minutes **Freeze:** No

For the Ramekins
25g dairy-free spread
25g unrefined caster sugar

Soufflés
200g best-quality (60% cocoa) dark, dairy-free chocolate, broken into pieces
25g dairy-free spread
2 tsp ground ginger
1 tsp ground mixed spice
½ tsp vanilla extract
2 tsp brandy
5 large eggs, separated
110g unrefined caster sugar
35g glacé ginger

TIP *It is very important to prepare the ramekins properly, so that the soufflé can climb up the sides of the dish in an even rise. Take your time and make sure the grease and sugar coating are evenly applied.*

Preheat the oven to 180°C/160°C fan/Gas 4.

Grease the ramekins with the dairy-free spread and coat the insides with the sugar. Place the ramekins on a baking sheet lined with foil and set aside.

Melt the chocolate, dairy-free spread, ground ginger, mixed spice, vanilla extract and brandy in a heatproof bowl set over a pan of barely simmering water, making sure the base of the bowl doesn't touch the water. Stir until combined, then take off the heat and remove the bowl from the pan.

Add the egg yolks one at a time and stir well to combine.

In a separate bowl, whisk the egg whites on a low speed, using an electric hand mixer, until they start to look frothy. Increase the speed to high and carefully add the sugar. The egg whites need to form a floppy meringue, a bit like shaving cream, so don't overdo the whisking.

Gently fold the meringue mixture and the glacé ginger into the chocolate soufflé base.

Carefully divide the mixture between the ramekins, leaving a space of at least 5mm at the top of each.

Transfer the baking sheet to the oven and bake for 10–11 minutes until the tops are firm around the edges and slightly soft and quivery in the middle.

Remove the soufflés from the oven and serve immediately with cold Rich and Creamy Vanilla Custard.

ORANGE AND GRAND MARNIER SOUFFLÉS

When baking a hot soufflé, it's important that you provide a sturdy climbing frame for the mixture or it won't rise up out of the dish, so grease your ramekins well and coat evenly with sugar. My soufflés don't have to rise uniformly – in fact, there is something to be said for the rustic informal approach with lots of quiver and wobble – but you do want them to get out of the starting blocks!

Serves: 4 **Equipment:** Four 250ml ramekins; electric hand mixer **Preparation time:** 45 minutes
Cooking time: Approx. 10–12 minutes **Freeze:** No

For the Ramekins
Dairy-free spread, for greasing
30g unrefined caster sugar

Soufflés
150ml freshly squeezed orange juice
1 tbsp lemon juice
25g wheat- and gluten-free
    plain flour
90g unrefined caster sugar
¼ tsp salt
160ml soya, rice, almond or
    coconut milk
4 large eggs, separated
30g dairy-free spread
Grated zest of 1 large orange
Grated zest of 1 large lemon
1 tbsp Grand Marnier

TIP *I like the soufflés on their own, but if you are serving them at a special lunch or dinner party, you can carefully crack the surface with a dessert spoon and pour in some cold crème anglaise flavoured with Grand Marnier (page 139), or a spoonful of Raspberry Coulis (page 143) if you are looking for a really fruity dessert.*

Boil the orange and lemon juice in a small saucepan until reduced to approximately 35ml; set aside. Preheat the oven to 200°C/180°C fan/Gas 6.

Grease the ramekins with dairy-free spread and coat the insides evenly with the sugar. Place on a baking sheet lined with foil and set aside.

Put the flour, 65g of the sugar and the salt in a medium heavy-based saucepan and quickly mix. Add about one third of the milk and, using a large wooden spoon, stir until smooth. Add the remaining milk and stir until combined.

Place over a low heat and stir constantly until the mixture thickens, 3–4 minutes. Remove from the heat and beat in the egg yolks and the dairy-free spread.

Return to the heat and continue stirring until a few bubbles appear on the surface. The mixture will become quite thick, but don't worry if it looks slightly lumpy.

Remove from the heat and pour through a fine metal sieve set over a large mixing bowl. Add the orange and lemon zest, stir to combine, then set aside for 10 minutes to cool.

Add the Grand Marnier and reduced orange juice and stir to combine.

In a separate bowl, using an electric hand mixer on a low speed, whisk the egg whites until they start to look frothy. Increase the speed to high and whisk in the remaining 25g sugar.

Fold half the meringue mixture into the soufflé base to loosen. Gently fold in the remaining half, taking care not to deflate the mix. Divide the mixture between the ramekins, leaving at least 5mm clear at the top.

Transfer the baking sheet to the oven and cook for 10–12 minutes or until the tops are light brown and slightly quivery. Serve immediately.

HOT CHOCOLATE SOUFFLÉS

This charming little soufflé isn't difficult to make and is lovely to serve at an informal supper party. I make the chocolate base in advance and store it in the fridge until needed. I can then quickly whisk the egg whites and fold them into the base, carefully pour into the ramekins, pop into the oven and voilà – a lovely light dessert designed to impress.

Serves: 6 **Equipment:** Six 250ml ramekins; electric hand mixer **Preparation time:** 1 hour
Cooking time: Approx. 15–17 minutes **Freeze:** No

For the Ramekins
Dairy-free spread, for greasing
10g cocoa powder

Soufflés
115g best-quality (60% cocoa) dark, dairy-free chocolate, broken into pieces
300ml coconut milk
2 tbsp water
40g dairy-free spread
40g wheat- and gluten-free plain flour
2–3 tsp dark rum, to taste
4 large eggs, separated
50g unrefined caster sugar
Icing sugar and cocoa powder, sifted, to dust

TIP *If you don't like the taste of coconut milk, this recipe works just as well with soya, rice, almond or hazelnut milk.*

Preheat the oven to 190°C/170°C fan/Gas 5.

Grease the ramekins with dairy-free spread and coat the insides evenly with the cocoa powder. Place on a baking sheet lined with foil.

Heat the chocolate, 2 tablespoons of the coconut milk and the water gently in a small heavy-based saucepan over a low heat. Stir until the chocolate has melted, then add the remaining coconut milk.

Gently melt the dairy-free spread in a medium saucepan, add the flour and quickly stir to combine. Don't worry if it clumps together, just heat for a minute or two, stirring constantly. Remove the pan from the heat and stir in the warm chocolate milk mixture, then return to the heat and bring to the boil, stirring constantly until thickened.

Remove from the heat and pour through a fine metal sieve set over a large heatproof bowl. Use the back of the wooden spoon to force the mixture through if it is thick, and to remove any lumps. Add the rum and leave the mixture to cool.

Beat the egg yolks one at a time into the cooled mixture and stir in the sugar.

In a separate bowl, on a low speed with an electric hand mixer, whisk the egg whites until they start to look frothy. Increase the speed to high and beat until they form a floppy meringue, a bit like shaving cream; don't overdo it.

Fold half the meringue mixture into the chocolate base to loosen. Gently fold in the remaining meringue mixture, taking care to keep as much air in as possible. Gently divide the mixture between the ramekins, leaving at least 5mm space above the mixture.

Transfer to the oven and cook for 15–17 minutes or until the tops are firm around the edges and slightly soft and quivery in the middle.

Dust lightly with icing sugar and cocoa powder and serve immediately.

SCOTTISH CHOCOLATE AND HAZELNUT CRANACHAN

Cranachan comes in many guises and was originally a Scottish celebration of harvest. Traditionally the ingredients were bought to the table separately so that each person could serve themselves, and whilst I love this informal approach, I prefer my cranachan to chill for a couple of hours in the fridge, allowing the flavours to develop and deepen.

Serves: 6 **Equipment:** Six individual serving glasses **Preparation time:** 30 minutes plus minimum 2 hours chilling **Cooking time:** Approx. 10 minutes **Freeze:** No

40g blanched hazelnuts
50g uncontaminated rolled oats
25g light muscovado sugar
100g best-quality (60% cocoa) dark, dairy-free chocolate, grated
300g fresh raspberries
1 tsp unrefined caster sugar
300ml coconut cream
100ml dairy-free sour cream
2 tbsp runny honey, plus extra to drizzle
4 tbsp malt whisky

Preheat the oven to 180°C/160°C fan/Gas 4. Spread the hazelnuts out on a baking tray and toast in the oven for 8–10 minutes until starting to brown. Tip onto a board and leave to cool, then roughly chop.

Heat the grill to its highest setting. Line a baking sheet with foil and spread the oats out evenly over it.

Grill the oats for a few minutes until golden brown, keeping a very close eye as they will burn, and stirring regularly to ensure even grilling. Tip into a large bowl.

Add the muscovado sugar, chopped hazelnuts and grated chocolate to the oats, stir well to combine and set aside.

In another bowl, lightly crush the raspberries, stir in the caster sugar and set aside.

Lightly whip the coconut cream, sour cream, honey and whisky together in a third bowl until light and fluffy.

Layer the 3 separate mixtures in the serving glasses, starting with the oat and chocolate mixture, followed by the raspberries and then the cream, repeating the process to give 6 layers, and reserving a little oat and chocolate mixture to serve. Chill in the fridge for at least 2 hours.

To serve, sprinkle with the reserved oat and chocolate mixture and add a light drizzle of honey to each.

TIP *The raspberries can be replaced with blackberries and the whisky with Drambuie for a slightly unorthodox, but equally delicious, version of the classic.*

RASPBERRY JAM ROLY-POLY

The addition of ground almonds in this recipe adds just enough lightness and richness to the pastry without changing the taste and texture too much. If, however, you are a pudding puritan or you don't like almonds, substitute them for the same weight in extra self-raising flour.

Serves: 6
Equipment: Roasting tin with rack
Preparation time: 20 minutes
Cooking time: 1 hour
Freeze: Yes – freeze uncooked and allow 1 hour defrosting time before steam-baking as indicated

Dairy-free spread, for greasing
150g wheat- and gluten-free self-raising flour, plus extra for dusting
100g ground almonds
1 tsp xanthan gum
¼ tsp salt
125g wheat- and gluten-free vegetarian suet
50g coconut palm sugar
8–10 tbsp water
3 heaped tbsp raspberry jam

TIP *Don't be tempted to put more jam in the roly-poly than recommended, as it will just seep out and make a mess. If you want a bit more sweetness, gently heat some extra jam in a small saucepan to pour over the cooked roly-poly.*

Preheat the oven to 200°C/180°C fan/Gas 6.

Cut out a sheet of baking parchment big enough to wrap your 30 x 20cm roly-poly in, and one the same size of foil. Lightly grease the baking parchment and set both aside.

Place a roasting rack in a roasting tin and fill with water to the level of the rack.

Sift the flour, ground almonds, xanthan gum and salt into a large mixing bowl, add the suet and sugar and mix together well. Add just enough water to create a soft, but not sticky, dough.

Place a large piece of clingfilm on a work surface and dust with flour. Turn the dough out onto the floured clingfilm and gently shape into a rectangle. Place another large piece of clingfilm over the top and, using a rolling pin, carefully start to roll the dough out into a rectangle about 20 x 30cm. Remove the top layer of clingfilm and, using a sharp knife, trim the edges of the dough to neaten.

Spread the jam evenly over the surface, leaving a 1cm clear border on 3 sides and a 2.5cm border on the short edge furthest from you (to prevent the jam spilling out when it is rolled).

Using the clingfilm underneath to help you, roll up the roly-poly tightly, starting from the short end nearest to you and ending with the join underneath. If any jam seeps out, scrape it off using a knife.

Lift the roly-poly onto the greased baking parchment, carefully sliding the clingfilm out from underneath. Roll up in the baking parchment, not too tightly as it will swell slightly during cooking. Secure the ends, then wrap in the foil, again not too tightly and securing the ends so that steam and water can't get in.

Gently place the wrapped roly-poly on the roasting rack and transfer the roasting tin to the oven.

Bake for 1 hour, then remove from the oven and leave to stand for 5 minutes before removing the foil and baking parchment, taking care of trapped steam escaping, which will be very hot.

Cut into slices and serve with lashings of warm Vanilla Custard.

SOUR CHERRY AND ALMOND CLAFOUTIS

Clafoutis is basically a French sweet Yorkshire pudding usually containing pitted fresh cherries, but because I like to serve this pudding in winter, I find frozen sour cherries work equally well. I also prefer to make a large pudding, but if you fancy making small ones in a Yorkshire pudding tin, then they will only need 10–15 minutes in the oven.

Serves: 6
Equipment: 25cm flan dish
Preparation time: 15 minutes
Cooking time: 35–40 minutes
Freeze: No

Dairy-free spread, for greasing
300g frozen sour cherries, defrosted
4 large eggs
225ml soya cream
225ml soya milk
½ vanilla pod
35g wheat- and gluten-free
   plain flour
40g ground almonds
Pinch of salt
75g unrefined caster sugar
25g flaked almonds
1 tbsp unrefined granulated sugar

Preheat the oven to 200°C/180°C fan/Gas 6. Generously grease the flan dish with dairy-free spread.

Spread the cherries evenly over the base of the flan dish.

Break the eggs into a large mixing bowl and add the cream and milk.

Using a sharp knife, scrape out the seeds from the half vanilla pod and add to the egg, cream and milk mixture. Beat well with a balloon whisk to combine.

Sift the flour, ground almonds and salt into the mixture, add the caster sugar and beat with a balloon whisk until combined.

Pour the mixture over the cherries and sprinkle the flaked almonds over the surface.

Place on a baking sheet and bake in the oven for 35–40 minutes until well risen, golden and firm.

Remove from the oven and sprinkle with the granulated sugar.

Serve warm with Coconut Cream or Madagascan Vanilla Ice Cream.

TIP *300g brandy-soaked stoned prunes make a delicious and rather decadent alternative to cherries.*

COCONUT SPICED BREAD PUDDING

The origins of bread pudding, not to be confused with bread and butter pudding, can be traced back as far as the 11th century, when frugal cooks made it as a way of using up stale, leftover bread. Wheat- and gluten-free breads work extremely well in this pudding and you don't have to wait for the bread to become stale before making it. The beauty of this pudding is its versatility; I really love tropical flavours, so have chosen coconut milk and coconut sugar spiked with rum, but you could just as easily swap these ingredients for soya or almond milk, whisky-soaked sultanas and light brown sugar, or add chocolate drops to the egg mixture after it has been heated.

Serves: 6
Equipment: Baking or pie dish, approx. 15 x 20cm; electric hand mixer
Preparation time: 30 minutes
Cooking time: 1¼ hours
Freeze: No

110g sultanas
50g raisins
50g currants
3 tbsp dark rum
225g wheat- and gluten-free white bread, crusts removed
275ml coconut milk
75g coconut sugar
2 tsp ground cinnamon
1 large egg, beaten
50g coconut oil, plus extra for greasing
Grated zest of 1 lemon
Grated zest of ½ orange
30g unrefined demerara sugar
Fresh nutmeg, for grating

Coconut and Rum Cream
400ml can coconut milk, chilled
½ tbsp icing sugar
2 tsp dark rum, or to taste

Preheat the oven to 180°C/160°C fan/Gas 4. Grease the baking dish with a little coconut oil.

Put the dried fruit in a bowl, pour over the rum and set aside to soak.

Tear the bread into small pieces, roughly 2.5cm, into a large bowl. Pour the coconut milk over, stir and leave to soak for 30 minutes.

Put the coconut sugar, cinnamon and beaten egg into another bowl. Gently melt the coconut oil in a small saucepan and add to the sugar mixture, stirring until combined.

Using a wooden spoon, beat the bread and milk mixture until smooth, then add the sugar mixture and beat until combined.

Stir in the dried fruit and any rum that might be left, then add the lemon and orange zest.

Pour into the greased baking dish and level the top using the back of a spoon. Sprinkle the surface with the demerara sugar; it might seem a lot, but you need it to create the crunchy top.

Bake for 1 hour 15 minutes until firm and golden, checking 5 minutes before the end of the cooking time and covering the pudding with foil if it is browning too much.

Meanwhile, to make the coconut and rum cream, turn the chilled can of coconut milk upside down. Open and remove the clear liquid, then spoon the remaining coconut cream into a mixing bowl; you need 120ml.

Add the icing sugar and rum to taste, and beat to soft peaks using an electric hand mixer. Chill in the fridge until needed, then serve with the hot pudding.

QUEEN OF PUDDINGS

This is a quintessentially English milk pudding that apparently wasn't invented for a queen at all. A similar pudding, called Monmouth Pudding, was first baked in the 17th century, and an identical pudding called Manchester Pudding was popular in the 19th century. Some food historians believe that the Manchester Pudding was renamed when Queen Victoria admired it on a visit to Manchester; however this pudding got its name, it is still very popular today. I like serving individual puddings, but it works equally well in a 1 litre ovenproof dish.

Serves: 6 **Equipment:** Six 115ml ramekins; electric hand mixer; piping bag fitted with an 806 stainless steel nozzle **Preparation time:** 20 minutes **Cooking time:** 25 minutes **Freeze:** No

50g dairy-free spread, plus extra
  for greasing
25g unrefined caster sugar
Grated zest of 1 lemon
400ml can coconut milk
Pinch of salt
150g wheat- and gluten-free white
  breadcrumbs
4 large eggs, separated (you will only
  need 2 whites)
4 tbsp Raspberry Ripple (page 149)
  or raspberry jam

Meringue
2 egg whites
50g unrefined caster sugar
2 tsp unrefined granulated sugar

Preheat the oven to 180°C/160°C fan/Gas 4. Lightly grease the ramekins with dairy-free spread and place on a baking sheet.

Put the 50g dairy-free spread, sugar, lemon zest, coconut milk and salt into a medium heavy-based saucepan and bring to a gentle simmer.

Remove from the heat and add the breadcrumbs. Leave to cool and thicken, stirring often, about 20 minutes.

Beat the egg yolks into the cooled breadcrumb mixture.

Spoon the mixture carefully into the greased ramekins and transfer to the oven for 15 minutes or until just set. The mixture will puff up quite a lot but will settle as it cools.

If using raspberry jam, warm it gently in a small saucepan.

Remove the puddings from the oven and very carefully spoon the Raspberry Ripple or warm jam over the surface of each pudding.

Using an electric hand mixer, whisk the egg whites to stiff peaks, then whisk in the caster sugar; don't over-whisk.

Spoon the meringue into a piping bag and pipe the meringue in a swirl on top of each pudding. Sprinkle evenly with the granulated sugar.

Cook in the oven for 8–10 minutes or until the meringue is lightly browned and crisp.

Leave for 5 minutes before serving.

TIP *If you want to make these puddings for a lunch or dinner party, you can bake them in advance, then keep them somewhere warm while you eat the main course.*

CHUNKY MARMALADE SPONGE

If you don't have two or three hours to spare for lovingly steaming a pudding for Sunday lunch, and you just happen to have a jar of Seville orange marmalade waiting to be used, then this is the perfect pudding for you. I love to serve it with a very grown-up Grand Marnier custard, but my Vanilla Custard works very nicely too.

Serves: 4–6
Equipment: 1 litre pudding basin; electric hand mixer
Preparation time: 20 minutes
Cooking time: 40–45 minutes
Freeze: No

175g orange marmalade, preferably Seville
150g dairy-free spread, plus extra for greasing
150g light muscovado sugar
Grated zest of 2 lemons
2 large eggs
2 tbsp soya, rice, almond or coconut milk
120g wheat- and gluten-free self-raising flour, sifted
1 tsp xanthan gum
1 tsp gluten-free baking powder
¼ tsp salt
30g ground almonds

Preheat the oven to 180°C/160°C fan/Gas 4. Lightly grease the pudding basin with dairy-free spread and line the base with a circle of baking parchment.

Gently warm the marmalade in a small saucepan, then pour it over the lined base and set aside to cool and settle.

Using an electric hand mixer, beat the dairy-free spread, sugar and lemon zest together until nice and fluffy.

Whisk the eggs and milk together, then add to the lemon and sugar mixture a little at a time, beating between additions.

Using a large metal spoon, gently fold in the flour, xanthan gum, baking powder, salt and ground almonds.

Carefully spoon the mixture into the basin over the marmalade and level the surface using the back of a spoon.

Bake in the oven for 40–45 minutes until beautifully puffed up and firm to the touch.

Leave to cool for 5 minutes in the basin, then carefully turn out onto a serving plate.

Serve with Grand Marnier or Vanilla Custard.

TIP *To ring the changes, this recipe works equally well with your favourite jam, golden syrup or stewed fruit in place of the marmalade.*

EVE'S PUDDING

Sometimes it's the simplest things in life that are the best, and this is certainly the case with Eve's Pudding. Unpretentious and often overlooked in favour of its more flamboyant sisters, this pudding is very easy to make. Full of delicious baked apples and topped with a light and fluffy vanilla sponge, my son Charlie and his friends absolutely adore it. I've recommended Bramley apples because I find they cook quickly and fluff up nicely, but if you want to use a different variety, you might find it best to slightly stew them first.

Serves: 6–8
Equipment: 2 litre casserole or pie dish; electric hand mixer
Preparation time: 30 minutes
Cooking time: 55–60 minutes
Freeze: No

800g Bramley apples
Grated zest and juice of 1 lemon
3 tbsp water
150g unrefined demerara sugar
150g dairy-free spread, plus extra
   for greasing
150g unrefined caster sugar
2 large eggs
1 tsp vanilla extract
150g wheat- and gluten-free
   self-raising flour, sifted
1 tsp xanthan gum
50g ground almonds
Icing sugar, sifted, to dust

Preheat the oven to 180°C/160°C fan/Gas 4. Lightly grease the casserole or pie dish with dairy-free spread and set aside.

Peel, core and thinly slice the apples and place in a large mixing bowl.

Add the lemon zest and juice, water and demerara sugar, making sure the apple slices are well coated, then transfer to the pie dish.

Using an electric hand mixer, beat the dairy-free spread and caster sugar together in a medium bowl until nice and fluffy.

Whisk the eggs and vanilla extract together before adding a little at a time to the spread and sugar mixture, beating until combined.

Using a large metal spoon, gently fold in the flour, xanthan gum and ground almonds.

Carefully spoon the mixture over the apples and level the surface using the back of the spoon; you don't need to be too neat, as a rustic look works really well.

Bake in the oven for 55–60 minutes or until the sponge is beautifully puffed up and firm to the touch especially in the centre.

Remove from the oven and leave to cool for 5 minutes before dusting lightly with icing sugar.

Serve with a scoop of Vanilla Ice Cream or lashings of Vanilla Custard.

TIP *If you don't need such a large pudding, just reduce the ingredients by half and use a 1 litre dish.*

HAZELNUT AND FRANGELICO BROWNIE POTS

I've lost count of how many emails I've received over the years from customers telling me how they love serving my award-winning brownies warm with a spoonful of ice cream. This gave me the idea of designing a brownie pudding that could be served straight from the oven with room for that all-important scoop on top. For anyone who knows me, it's not surprising that I've chosen to add hazelnuts, my favourite nuts, and a dash of lovely, warming Frangelico. Don't forget to use the best-quality dairy-free chocolate with a minimum of 60% cocoa solids.

Serves: 8
Equipment: Eight 180ml ramekins or ovenproof cups; electric hand mixer
Preparation time: 45 minutes
Cooking time: Approx. 35 minutes
Freeze: Yes – defrost to room temperature, then reheat until warm

50g blanched hazelnuts, roughly chopped, plus extra to decorate
185g best-quality (60% cocoa) dark, dairy-free chocolate, broken into pieces
185g dairy-free spread
3 large eggs
275g unrefined caster sugar
2 tsp espresso powder
2 tbsp Frangelico
85g wheat- and gluten-free plain flour, sifted
1 tsp xanthan gum
40g cocoa powder, sifted
½ tsp salt

Preheat the oven to 180°C/160°C fan/Gas 4.

Place the hazelnuts on a baking sheet and toast for 6–8 minutes until golden brown.

Remove the nuts from the oven and set aside to cool.

Lower the oven temperature to 170°C/150°C fan/Gas 3.

Place the ramekins or ovenproof cups on a baking sheet.

Melt the chocolate and dairy-free spread together in a heatproof bowl. You can either do this over a saucepan of barely simmering water on the hob, making sure the base of the bowl doesn't touch the water, or, like me, in the microwave on a high setting for about 1½ minutes. Stir until well mixed.

In a large bowl, using an electric hand mixer on a high speed, beat the eggs, sugar, espresso powder and Frangelico together until thick and creamy, about 3 minutes.

Gradually add the melted chocolate mixture on a slow mixer speed until well combined.

Gently fold in the sifted flour, xanthan gum, cocoa powder and salt, using long folding motions; you don't want to beat the air out.

Divide the mixture into the ramekins or ovenproof cups, then roughly chop the toasted hazelnuts and sprinkle evenly over each pot. Gently push the nuts down into the mixture until well hidden.

Bake the pots in the preheated oven for 25 minutes. You might think they don't look cooked and be tempted to leave them in for longer, but don't, as brownies continue to cook and firm as they cool.

Leave the pots to cool down for 15–20 minutes before serving so that the brownies are warm and gooey.

Serve with a scoop of Vanilla Ice Cream on top.

CHRISTMAS CRUMBLE

Who doesn't love a crumble? Just the thought of one puts a smile on my face, but the success of this crumble really does depend upon the quality of your mincemeat. Ideally, you should use my Cranberry and Port Mincemeat (page 151), but if you don't have time to make your own, choose one with a low sugar content and add a dash of booze, just to give your pudding a hint of luxury.

Serves: 6–8 **Equipment:** 2 litre ovenproof dish; food processor (optional) **Preparation time:** 20 minutes
Cooking time: 35–45 minutes **Freeze:** Yes – Cool the cooked crumble to room temperature, cover with clingfilm and foil and freeze for up to 3 months. Defrost overnight in the fridge, remove the clingfilm, cover with foil and reheat for 30 minutes, or until hot, at 190°C/170°C fan/Gas 5

50g blanched hazelnuts
400g firm pears
Grated zest and juice of 1 orange
600g best-quality mincemeat
5 dairy-, wheat- and gluten-free
　ginger biscuits
200g wheat- and gluten-free
　plain flour
1 tsp xanthan gum
100g dairy-free spread, cubed
100g light muscovado sugar

TIP *I love hazelnuts, but this recipe works just as well with walnuts or toasted pecan nuts.*

Preheat the oven to 200°C/180°C fan/Gas 6.

Spread the hazelnuts out on a baking tray and toast for 6–8 minutes or until golden brown. Tip onto a plate and set aside to cool.

Peel and core the pears, cut into 1cm cubes and put into the ovenproof dish. Add the orange zest and juice, then add the mincemeat and stir well to combine.

Break the ginger biscuits into small pieces and blitz to crumbs in a food processor. Alternatively, place the biscuits in a small freezer bag and crush with a rolling pin.

Add the flour, xanthan gum and dairy-free spread cubes to the biscuit crumbs and process until the mixture resembles coarse breadcrumbs. Alternatively, put all the ingredients in a large mixing bowl and rub the spread in using your fingertips.

Roughly chop the toasted hazelnuts and add with the sugar to the crumble mixture.

Sprinkle the crumble mixture evenly over the mincemeat and pears and bake in the oven for 35–40 minutes or until golden and bubbling.

Serve with lots of Vanilla Ice Cream or Vanilla Custard.

BASK IN THE UNSTINTING
ADMIRATION OF FAMILY
AND FRIENDS WITH THE
MOST SERIOUSLY DELICIOUS
CHEESECAKES, TRIFLES,
MOUSSES AND MERINGUES;
PERFECT FOR SUPPER WITH
FRIENDS, BIRTHDAY TEA TREATS
OR DESPERATE-TO-IMPRESS
DINNER PARTIES.

Chilled Desserts

ROASTED GOOSEBERRY, GINGER AND ELDERFLOWER CHEESECAKE

This recipe belongs to my grandmother May, who grew gooseberry bushes. For years my mother believed she had been found beneath a gooseberry bush, a bit like arriving by stork, and the phrase was frequently used in our family when celebrating a new arrival. I spent many happy hours topping and tailing gooseberries for May's bakes, but her cheesecake was always my favourite.

Serves: 6 **Equipment:** 23cm loose-bottomed flan tin; food processor (optional); electric hand mixer
Preparation time: 30 minutes plus resting and at least 2 hours cooling, preferably overnight **Cooking time:** Approx.
1¼ hours **Freeze:** Yes — open freeze until solid, then wrap in foil and freeze in a rigid container for up to 2 months

Base
200g dairy-, wheat- and gluten-free
  ginger biscuits
75g dairy-free block margarine
  or coconut butter, plus extra
  for greasing
30g unrefined demerara sugar

Filling
500g fresh or frozen gooseberries,
  defrosted
50g unrefined caster sugar
300g dairy-free cream cheese,
  at room temperature
1 tbsp wheat- and gluten-free
  plain flour
1 large egg plus 1 large yolk
1½ tbsp elderflower cordial
75ml dairy-free sour cream,
  at room temperature
Finely grated zest of 1 large lemon

Topping
260ml dairy-free sour cream
2½ tbsp elderflower cordial
Handful of fresh, or frozen and
  thawed, gooseberries, to decorate

Preheat the oven to 170°C/150°C fan/Gas 3. Grease the base and sides of the flan tin.

Pulse the biscuits in a food processor until they resemble sand. Alternatively, finely crush them in a freezer bag using a rolling pin. Melt the dairy-free margarine or coconut butter in a large heavy-based saucepan, then stir in the biscuit crumbs and demerara sugar. Firmly press into the base and up the sides of the flan tin; this can be fiddly.

Bake in the oven for 10 minutes, then leave to cool for at least 15 minutes. Increase the oven temperature to 200°C/180°C fan/Gas 6.

Place the gooseberries in a roasting tin lined with baking parchment, sprinkle with the caster sugar and mix. Roast for 15–20 minutes until soft but not completely broken down. Transfer to a sieve over a large bowl and leave to drain. Reduce the oven to 180°C/160°C fan/Gas 4.

Put the cream cheese, flour, egg and yolk, elderflower cordial, sour cream and lemon zest into a large bowl and beat with an electric hand mixer until smooth; don't over-beat. Pour into the biscuit base. Place on a baking sheet and bake in the oven for 30 minutes, then cool.

Meanwhile, pour the drained gooseberry juice into a small pan, bring to the boil and gently boil until reduced to approx. 1 tablespoon. Put a handful of gooseberries in a small bowl and set aside. Place the remainder of the berries in a bowl, add the tablespoon of gooseberry syrup and mash lightly before spooning over the cooled cheesecake.

To make the topping, beat the sour cream and cordial with a balloon whisk, then pour slowly over the gooseberries in the tin. Return to the oven for a further 15 minutes, then turn the oven off and leave the cheesecake in to cool for at least 2 hours, but preferably overnight.

To serve, top with the reserved roasted gooseberries.

ESPRESSO AND HAZELNUT BAKED CHEESECAKE

Since discovering I could make truly delicious dairy-free cheesecakes, I have become slightly obsessed. The flavour combinations are seemingly endless and, whilst the Traditional Manhattan Cheesecake (page 91) will always be my favourite, the combination of chocolate, coffee and hazelnut comes a very close second.

Serves: 10–12 **Equipment:** 23cm springform cake tin; food processor; electric hand mixer
Preparation time: 45 minutes plus minimum 4 hours chilling, preferably overnight **Cooking time:** 45–60 minutes
Freeze: Yes – open freeze until solid, then wrap in foil and freeze in a rigid container for up to 2 months

---

Base
90g blanched hazelnuts
230g dairy-, wheat- and gluten-free digestive biscuits
110g coconut butter or dairy-free block margarine, plus extra for greasing
75g best-quality (60% cocoa) dark, dairy-free chocolate, chopped

Filling
175g best-quality (60% cocoa) dark, dairy-free chocolate, chopped
500g dairy-free cream cheese, at room temperature
150g dairy-free sour cream, at room temperature
1 tbsp wheat- and gluten-free plain flour
230g unrefined soft light brown sugar, sifted to remove lumps
3 large eggs plus 3 large yolks, beaten
1 tsp vanilla extract
75ml espresso coffee, cooled

Preheat the oven to 180°C/160°C fan/Gas 4. Grease and line the base of the springform cake tin.

Spread the hazelnuts evenly out on a baking tray and toast in the oven for 6–8 minutes until starting to brown. Tip onto a plate to cool.

Put the biscuits and cooled hazelnuts into a food processor and pulse until they resemble fine breadcrumbs. Melt the coconut butter or dairy-free margarine and chocolate together in a large heavy-based saucepan over a gentle heat. Add the biscuit and hazelnut crumbs and stir thoroughly.

Press the biscuit mixture into the base of the lined tin and chill in the freezer for about 30 minutes.

Meanwhile, melt the chocolate for the filling in a heatproof bowl set over a saucepan of barely simmering water, making sure the base of the bowl doesn't touch the water, and set aside to cool.

In a large bowl, use an electric hand mixer to beat the cream cheese until nice and smooth. Add the sour cream, flour, sugar, eggs and yolks and vanilla and beat until combined, 3–4 minutes. Beat in the coffee and melted chocolate.

Remove the cake tin from the freezer and carefully wrap with 2 layers of clingfilm and a sheet of foil (to make it watertight). Boil the kettle.

Sit the wrapped cake tin in a roasting tin and pour in the cheesecake filling. Pour boiling water into the roasting tin to come halfway up the sides of the cheesecake tin. Carefully transfer to the oven and bake for 45–60 minutes; the top of the cheesecake should be set but have a slight wobble. Remove from the roasting tin and leave to cool.

Cover with clingfilm and chill in the fridge for a minimum of 4 hours, but preferably overnight. Serve cut into slices.

TRADITIONAL MANHATTAN CHEESECAKE

Served in every deli, café, tea room and restaurant around the world, this iconic cheesecake was always one of my favourite treats and one I thought I would never have again. For years I tinkered with various recipes, but they just never tasted quite right, or I couldn't get them to set properly. And then I had a eureka moment... I tried a different brand of dairy-free cream cheese (see page 10). It worked. I was so excited I made another one with normal cream cheese and asked friends to blind test them; they all preferred the dairy-free one.

Serves: 10–12 **Equipment:** 23cm springform cake tin; food processor (optional); electric hand mixer
Preparation time: 25 minutes plus 2 hours cooling and overnight chilling **Cooking time:** 45 minutes
Freeze: Yes – open freeze until solid, then wrap in foil and freeze in a rigid container for up to 2 months

---

Base
175g dairy-, wheat- and gluten-free
   digestive biscuits
55g coconut butter or dairy-free
   block margarine, plus extra
   for greasing
30g unrefined demerara sugar

Filling
1kg dairy-free cream cheese,
   at room temperature
250g unrefined caster sugar
3 tsp wheat- and gluten-free
   plain flour
1 tsp vanilla extract
Finely grated zest and juice of
   1 lemon
Finely grated zest of 1 orange
3 large eggs, beaten
300ml dairy-free sour cream,
   at room temperature

Topping
150ml dairy-free sour cream
1 tbsp unrefined caster sugar
Berries and edible flowers (optional)

TIP *I love serving this with a drizzle of either Raspberry or Damson Coulis (page 143).*

Preheat the oven to 180°C/160°C fan/Gas 4. Grease the base and sides of the cake tin.

Pulse the biscuits in a food processor until they resemble sand. Alternatively, finely crush them in a freezer bag using a rolling pin. Melt the coconut butter or margarine in a large heavy-based saucepan, then stir in the biscuit crumbs and demerara sugar. Firmly press the mixture into the base of the tin.

Bake in the oven for 10 minutes, then leave to cool. Increase the oven temperature to 220°C/200°C fan/Gas 7.

In a large mixing bowl, use an electric hand mixer to beat the cream cheese until creamy. Gradually beat in the sugar and then the flour. Beat in the vanilla extract, lemon zest and juice and orange zest, then gradually beat in the eggs.

Slowly beat in the sour cream on a low speed until the mixture is smooth and light. Pour the filling on top of the biscuit base, keeping the surface as smooth as possible.

Bake in the oven for 10 minutes, then reduce the oven temperature to 150°C/130°C fan/Gas 2 and bake for a further 25 minutes. It will appear very wobbly, but this is fine. Switch off the oven and leave the cheesecake in the oven with the door closed for 2 hours. The top may be cracked and the cheesecake still wobbly, but don't worry.

To make the topping, use the electric hand mixer to beat the sour cream and caster sugar together until nicely creamy. Spread the mixture over the top of the cheesecake, right to the edge, before chilling in the fridge overnight.

Remove from the tin and top with berries and edible flowers if you like.

QUICK AND EASY LEMON CHEESECAKE

This might not be a traditional and lovingly baked cheesecake, but it is delicious nonetheless. To add to its appeal, it can be thrown together in a fraction of the time of its more established brethren. If you don't have time to make your own Blackcurrant Ripple, use a really good-quality conserve that is low in sugar.

Serves: 8–10
Equipment: 20cm springform cake tin; food processor (optional); electric hand mixer
Preparation time: 15 minutes plus minimum 4 hours cooling, preferably overnight
Freeze: Yes – open freeze until solid, then wrap in foil and freeze in a rigid container for up to 2 months

Base
125g dairy-, wheat- and gluten-free digestive biscuits
75g dairy-free block margarine or coconut butter, plus extra for greasing
25g unrefined demerara sugar

Filling
300g dairy-free cream cheese, at room temperature
60g icing sugar, sifted
1 tsp vanilla extract
Finely grated zest of 2 large lemons and 1 tsp juice
250ml coconut cream

Topping
½ quantity Blackcurrant Ripple (page 142) or 250g good-quality blackcurrant conserve

Lightly grease the base and sides of the springform tin.

Pulse the biscuits in a food processor until they resemble sand. Alternatively, finely crush them in a freezer bag using a rolling pin.

Melt the dairy-free margarine or coconut butter in a large heavy-based saucepan. Remove from the heat and stir in the biscuit crumbs and demerara sugar.

Firmly and evenly press the mixture into the base of the tin then chill in the fridge to firm.

To make the filling, use an electric hand mixer to beat the cream cheese until nicely soft.

Add the icing sugar, vanilla extract and lemon zest and juice and beat until combined.

Lightly whip the coconut cream in a separate bowl and, using a large metal spoon, fold into the cheese mixture.

Spoon the filling onto the chilled biscuit base and smooth it out using the back of a spoon. Return to the fridge for at least 4 hours, but preferably overnight.

To serve, very carefully remove the cheesecake from the tin. Spoon the Blackcurrant Ripple or conserve on top and very gently smooth to the edges. Use a long, sharp knife dipped in hot water to cut into slices.

TIRAMISU

This is a real blast from the past that still tastes exceptionally good today. Over the years I have searched high and low for a dairy-, wheat- and gluten-free alternative to lady's fingers, but to no avail, so to keep my options open, I try to keep a bag of homemade ones in the freezer, then with a bit of forethought and a carton of ready-made custard I can have a Tiramisù chilling in the fridge within 30 minutes.

Serves: 4
Equipment: Electric hand mixer; serving dish, ideally glass
Preparation time: 20 minutes plus minimum 3 hours chilling (the longer the better)
Freeze: No

225g dairy-free cream cheese, at room temperature
50g dairy-free sour cream
60g coconut cream
250g shop-bought dairy-free custard
½ tsp vanilla extract
3 tbsp Marsala or brandy
1 tbsp unrefined icing sugar
150ml espresso, cooled
16–18 Lady's Fingers (page 152)
1 tbsp cocoa powder
25g best-quality (60% cocoa) dark, dairy-free chocolate, shaved into curls

Put the cream cheese, sour cream, coconut cream, custard, vanilla extract, Marsala or brandy, icing sugar and 1 tablespoon of the cold espresso into a large mixing bowl. Using an electric hand mixer, beat for a couple of minutes until light, smooth and creamy.

Dip one third of the Lady's Fingers into the remaining espresso, making sure not to get them too soggy, then use to line the base of the serving dish, packing them in and if necessary, cutting them in half so they fit snugly. Tiramisù is as much about the coffee-soaked sponge as the Marsala-flavoured cream.

Spoon over one third of the cream mixture, then sprinkle with some of the cocoa powder.

Repeat the process with second and third layers.

Chill in the fridge for at least 3 hours, but longer if you can so that the flavours really get a chance to develop.

Remove from the fridge and sprinkle with chocolate curls.

TIP *If chocolate curls are proving elusive, you can grate the chocolate over the top or sift 2 tablespoons cocoa powder.*

LORNA'S CRANBERRY TORTE WITH ORANGE, HONEY AND STAR ANISE SYRUP

This is one of my husband's favourite puds. The recipe came from his mother, who was Australian, who got it from an American friend, who got it from another friend... But never mind all that. It's really delicious, simple to make and everyone in our family loves it!

Serves: 8–10
Equipment: 23cm springform cake tin
Preparation time: 20 minutes
Cooking time: 1 hour
Freeze: No

290g wheat- and gluten-free
   plain flour
1 tsp xanthan gum
1 tsp gluten-free baking powder
1 tsp bicarbonate of soda
½ tsp salt
285g unrefined caster sugar
115g walnuts, chopped
115g dates, stoned and chopped
230g cranberries, fresh or frozen
Finely grated zest and juice of
   2 large oranges
2 large eggs
140ml soya or coconut yoghurt
230ml water
170ml sunflower oil, plus extra
   for greasing

Orange, Honey and Star Anise Syrup
200ml orange juice
100g runny honey
1 star anise

Preheat the oven to 180°C/160°C fan/Gas 4. Grease the cake tin with a little oil and line with baking parchment.

Sift the flour, xanthan gum, baking powder, bicarbonate of soda and salt into a large bowl.

Add 235g of the sugar, the chopped walnuts and dates, cranberries (don't worry about defrosting if frozen) and orange zest.

In a separate bowl, beat the eggs, yoghurt, water and oil together, then add to the flour and fruit mixture and stir to combine.

Pour the mixture into the cake tin, level the top and bake for 1 hour or until a metal skewer inserted into the middle comes out clean.

Meanwhile, mix the orange juice from the zested oranges with the remaining 50g caster sugar.

Remove the torte from the oven and prick the surface all over with a skewer. Slowly drizzle the orange juice and sugar mixture over the surface of the torte; there's a lot, so it will take a while to soak in. Leave to cool.

To make the Orange, Honey and Star Anise Syrup, put the orange juice, honey and star anise in a small heavy-based pan and bring to a low boil. Simmer until reduced by half and the mixture is thick and syrupy. Remove from the heat, transfer to a jug and leave to cool. Once cool, remove the star anise, cover and store in the fridge until needed.

Serve the torte warm or cold with the syrup and some whipped coconut cream.

APRICOT FOOL WITH ORANGE POLENTA BISCUITS

Luxurious, rich, creamy and completely delicious, it really is hard to believe this summer fool is not made from double cream. I love to use the little Hunza apricots, which aren't much to look at but taste absolutely divine, but if you can't find these, you can use dried apricots (the ones that haven't been preserved with sulphur dioxide).

Serves: 6 (makes 30–40 biscuits)
Equipment: Food processor; electric hand mixer; 5cm round biscuit cutter; 6 glass serving dishes or glasses
Preparation time: 30 minutes plus 1 hour soaking
Cooking time: Approx. 1 hour
Freeze: Yes – freeze the fool for 4–6 weeks and the biscuits for 3 months

Apricot Fool

250g Hunza apricots or
    175g dried apricots
1½ tsp vanilla extract
Juice of ½ lemon
Juice of 1 orange
2 x 400ml cans coconut milk,
    chilled for 24 hours
½ tbsp icing sugar

Orange Polenta Biscuits

75g coarse polenta
25g rice flour, plus extra for dusting
25g ground almonds
¾ tsp gluten-free baking powder
75g icing sugar
50g dairy-free spread, cut into
    small cubes
1 large egg yolk, beaten
Grated zest of 1 orange
30g toasted flaked almonds, to serve

Put the apricots in a medium saucepan, add cold water to cover and leave to soak for 1 hour, then bring to a low simmer and cook for 45 minutes or until starting to fall apart and the remaining couple of tablespoons of water are a thin syrup. Remove from the heat and leave to cool for 20 minutes.

Remove the stones from the apricots, if using Hunza. Transfer the apricots to a food processor, add 1 teaspoon of the vanilla extract with the lemon and orange juice and blitz until smooth.

Turn the chilled cans of coconut milk upside down, open and drain the liquid out. Spoon 350ml of the remaining cream into a large bowl, add the remaining ½ teaspoon vanilla extract and the icing sugar and beat with an electric hand mixer just to soft peaks.

Fold the apricot mixture lightly into the coconut cream, spoon into the serving dishes or glasses and chill in the fridge. Preheat the oven to 180°C/160°C fan/Gas 4.

To make the biscuits, blitz the polenta, rice flour, ground almonds, baking powder, icing sugar and cubed dairy-free spread to the texture of fine breadcrumbs in the cleaned-out food processor. Add the egg yolk and orange zest and blitz again until the mixture forms a ball.

Place a large piece of clingfilm on your work surface and dust with rice flour. Turn the dough onto the clingfilm and flatten into a disc, before covering with another large piece of clingfilm.

Using a large rolling pin, roll the dough out into an even, thin disc, then remove the top sheet of clingfilm.

Stamp out 30–40 biscuits with the biscuit cutter (taking care, as the dough is fragile) and, using a palette knife, lift onto 2 baking sheets lined with baking parchment, allowing room for the biscuits to spread.

Bake in the oven for 6–8 minutes or until golden. Leave on the baking sheets for a few minutes before transferring to a wire rack to cool.

Sprinkle the fools with the toasted almonds and serve with the biscuits.

BOOZY CHOCOLATE, RASPBERRY AND COCONUT TRIFLE POTS

Trifle always reminds me of afternoon tea at my Granny's; sponge, jelly, fruit and custard being the perfect pudding for a child. These, however, are very grown-up trifles – soft and rich with a hint of booze, and served in individual pots. I love making these for a dinner party, as I can mostly prepare them the day before and they look great served in my collection of retro jam jars.

Serves: 6
Equipment: 20cm round, deep cake tin; electric hand mixer; biscuit cutters; six 370g vintage jam jars or glass dishes
Preparation time: Approx. 1 hour plus 30 minutes cooling and 30 minutes to assemble
Cooking time: 15–20 minutes
Freeze: No

3 tbsp dessert wine
1 quantity Chocolate Crème
  Pâtissière (page 147)
Handful of fresh raspberries
1 quantity Raspberry Coulis
  (page 143)
1 quantity Coconut Cream
  (page 138)
50g toasted coconut chips, to serve
Chocolate Genoise
55g dairy-free spread, plus extra
  for greasing
4 large egg yolks, at room
  temperature
125g unrefined caster sugar
85g wheat- and gluten-free
  plain flour
½ tsp xanthan gum
30g cocoa powder

Preheat the oven to 190°C/170°C fan/Gas 5. Grease the cake tin and line with baking parchment.

For the genoise, gently melt the dairy-free spread in a small heavy-based saucepan, then remove from the heat and leave to cool.

Put the egg yolks and sugar into a heatproof bowl and set it over a saucepan of just-boiled water. Using an electric mixer, whisk together until light, thick and fluffy, about 10 minutes.

Remove the bowl from the pan and beat for a further 2 minutes until the mixture leaves a ribbon trail when the whisk is lifted; do not over-whisk. Using a large metal spoon, quickly but gently fold in the melted dairy-free spread.

Sift in the flour, xanthan gum and cocoa powder and quickly and gently fold in. Spoon the mixture into the prepared tin and tap lightly on the work surface to remove any large air pockets.

Bake in the centre of the oven for 15–20 minutes or until the cake is just coming away from the sides of the tin. Leave to cool in the tin.

To assemble the trifles, carefully slice the cake in half horizontally using a bread knife. Using round biscuit cutters, cut out 6 rounds in 2 different sizes to fit snuggly in the jam jars or serving dishes. Cut them in half horizontally again so that you have 12 thin slices. Place the rounds in a large dish for now and sprinkle with the dessert wine.

Place the smaller rounds in the base of the jars or dishes and spoon 2 heaped teaspoons of Chocolate Crème Pâtissière over the top of the cake. Place about 6 raspberries on the Crème Pâtissière. Place the larger rounds of cake on top and press down firmly.

Spoon another 2 heaped teaspoons of Chocolate Crème Pâtissière on top of the cake and pour a layer of Raspberry Coulis over the top, followed by a generous covering of Coconut Cream. Sprinkle the toasted coconut chips over the top. Chill until needed.

CHOCOLATE, PRUNE AND ARMAGNAC TORTE

When is a cake a torte? Apparently, the word comes from the Spanish and Italian 'torta', meaning 'round bread or cake', and in Europe cakes are commonly referred to as 'tortes' (although in France they can also be called 'gâteaux'). During my culinary travels, I have found that tortes are generally richer and more luxurious than your average cake, are often soaked in liqueur and contain ground nuts for added density and flavour. This chocolate dessert is a wonderful example of a European torte, rich in flavour but light in touch – in other words, perfect.

Serves: 6–8
Equipment: 23cm springform cake tin; electric hand mixer
Preparation time: 30 minutes
Cooking time: 30–35 minutes
Freeze: No

240g best-quality (60% cocoa) dark, dairy-free chocolate, chopped
200g dairy-free spread, plus extra for greasing
5 large eggs, separated
100g unrefined caster sugar
125g Prunes Soaked in Armagnac (page 153 or see TIP opposite)
¼ tsp salt
150g ground almonds

Preheat the oven to 180°C/160°C fan/Gas 4. Grease the cake tin with dairy-free spread and line with baking parchment.

Melt the chocolate and the dairy-free spread in a heatproof bowl set over a pan of barely simmering water, making sure the base of the bowl doesn't touch the water or the chocolate will seize.

Remove the bowl from the pan and leave to cool slightly.

Put the egg yolks in a bowl, add half the sugar and, using an electric hand mixer, beat until the mixture thickens, then fold into the melted chocolate mixture.

Remove the stones from the prunes, then chop into small pieces and add to the chocolate mixture, along with the salt and ground almonds.

Whisk the egg whites in a clean bowl with the remaining sugar, using the cleaned electric hand mixer, until soft peaks form. Using a large metal spoon, carefully fold the whites into the chocolate mixture until just combined.

Pour the mixture into the prepared cake tin and bake for 30–35 minutes. The torte needs to be slightly wobbly in the middle, so don't over-bake it.

Leave the torte to cool for 15 minutes before removing from the tin. I like to serve it at room temperature when it has firmed slightly, but it tastes equally delicious served warm and gooey, with softly whipped coconut cream to counter-balance the richness.

TIP *If you don't have a supply of prunes already soaking in a jar of brandy or Armagnac, soak the prunes in 40ml Armagnac for several hours, but preferably overnight.*

BANOFFEE FOOLS

Wonderfully quick and easy to make, these are totally addictive and adored by all.

Serves: 6
Equipment: Electric hand mixer; food processor (optional); 6 glass serving tumblers
Preparation time: 20 minutes plus chilling
Freeze: No

1 quantity Coconut Cream (page 138)
8 dairy-, wheat- and gluten-free stem ginger biscuits
30g best-quality (60% cocoa) dark, dairy-free chocolate, plus a little extra, grated, to serve
2 large bananas
1 tbsp lemon juice
3 tbsp Caramel Sauce (page 108)
275g ready-made dairy-free custard

Make the Coconut Cream and chill in the fridge.

Pulse the ginger biscuits in a food processor until they resemble sand (you will be left with small chunks of stem ginger, but this just adds a lovely chewy element). Alternatively, put the biscuits in a freezer bag and lightly crush them using a rolling pin.

Melt the chocolate in a small heatproof bowl set over a saucepan of barely simmering water, making sure the base of the bowl doesn't touch the water or the chocolate will seize.

Stir the crushed biscuits into the melted chocolate until combined, and set aside.

Slice the bananas, put them in a bowl and toss with the lemon juice. Stir in the Caramel Sauce.

Remove the Coconut Cream from the fridge and fold the custard into it.

To assemble, spoon 1 tablespoon biscuit mixture into the base of each serving tumbler, then divide half the banana and caramel mixture between them, followed by half the coconut cream and custard mixture.

Repeat the layers, then sprinkle the tops with a little grated chocolate and serve immediately.

BANANA AND TOFFEE-FILLED BROWN SUGAR MERINGUES WITH COCONUT CREAM AND CRUNCHY PEANUT BRITTLE

It's terribly chic these days to serve your guests light and fluffy meringues for dessert. I love to pile them high on a platter with the whipped cream, toffee sauce, banana and peanut brittle served alongside, then everyone can have fun helping themselves. It's always a hit and I never have any left over!

Serves: 6
Equipment: Electric hand mixer
Preparation time: 30 minutes
Cooking time: 1¼–1½ hours
Freeze: Yes – freeze the cooked meringues in a rigid plastic container, then defrost at room temperature

Meringue
4 large egg whites
Pinch of salt
115g light muscovado sugar
115g unrefined icing sugar

Toffee Filling
20g dairy-free spread
40g unrefined soft light brown sugar
20g unrefined caster sugar
60g golden syrup
60ml coconut cream
¼ tsp vanilla extract

To Serve
1 large banana
A little freshly squeezed lemon juice
1 quantity Coconut Cream
  (page 138)
1 quantity Peanut Brittle (page 155),
  finely crushed

Preheat the oven to 120°C/100°C fan/Gas ¼. Line a large baking sheet with baking parchment.

In a large, clean metal or glass bowl, and using an electric hand mixer, whisk the egg whites and salt until they hold soft peaks. Continue whisking as you gradually add the light muscovado sugar, a tablespoon at a time.

Sift a third of the icing sugar over the meringue mixture and, using a large metal spoon, gently fold in. Continue to sift and fold in the remaining icing sugar a third at a time until the meringue is nice and smooth.

Dollop 12 dessertspoonfuls of meringue onto the baking sheet in rough rounds, making sure to leave space in between each.

Bake in the oven for 1 hour 30 minutes if you are using a fan oven, or 1 hour 15 minutes in a conventional or gas oven, or until the meringues sound crisp when tapped underneath. Leave to cool on the baking sheet.

While the meringues are in the oven, to make the toffee sauce, gently melt the dairy-free spread with the sugars and golden syrup in a small heavy-based saucepan.

Stirring, bring the mixture to a gentle boil, then reduce the heat and simmer for 3–4 minutes. Remove from the heat and stir in the coconut cream and vanilla extract. Pour into a jug and leave to cool for a few minutes before covering and placing in the fridge to chill and thicken.

To serve, thinly slice the banana and toss in lemon juice. Remove the toffee filling from the fridge and either sandwich 2 meringues together with a generous layer of toffee filling, sliced banana and Coconut Cream, sprinkled with finely crushed Peanut Brittle, or pile the meringues onto a platter and serve the fillings alongside.

MINI PAVLOVAS WITH COFFEE AND KAHLUA ICE CREAM AND BLACKCURRANT COMPOTE

This pudding has to be one of my all-time favourites. The sweetness of the meringue, the complex nuttiness of the coffee and the tart and musky flavour of the blackcurrants all come together in one totally delicious taste sensation, and best of all it's simple to make.

Serves: 6
Equipment: Electric hand mixer
Preparation time: 30 minutes plus 30 minutes cooling
Cooking time: Approx. 40 minutes
Freeze: Yes – freeze the cooked meringues in a rigid plastic container and defrost at room temperature. Freeze the blackcurrant compote in a freezer bag or plastic container and defrost at room temperature

Meringue
4 large egg whites
Pinch of salt
200g unrefined caster sugar
1 tsp cornflour
1 tsp white wine vinegar
1 tsp coffee extract

Blackcurrant Compote
400g fresh or frozen blackcurrants
4 tbsp runny honey

To Serve
50g blanched hazelnuts
1 quantity Coffee and Kahlúa Ice Cream (page 121)

Preheat the oven to 180°C/160°C fan/Gas 4. Spread the hazelnuts out on a baking tray and toast in the oven for 6–8 minutes until golden brown. Tip onto a board, roughly chop and leave to cool.

Line 2 baking sheets with baking parchment and draw three 10cm diameter circles on each sheet, leaving space in between each (for the meringues to spread). Turn the parchment over so that the pencil markings are underneath, but visible.

In a large, clean metal or glass bowl, and using an electric hand mixer, whisk the egg whites and salt together until they hold soft peaks. Continue whisking while gradually adding the sugar, a tablespoon at a time.

Using a large metal spoon, gently fold in the cornflour, vinegar and coffee extract until just combined.

Dollop 6 large spoonfuls of meringue onto the marked circles. Use a spatula to roughly smooth the mixture out, creating a slight dip in the centre of each where the ice cream will sit.

Transfer to the oven and immediately reduce the oven temperature to 150°C/130°C fan/Gas 2. Bake for 30 minutes, then turn the oven off and leave the pavlovas in the oven to cool for a further 30 minutes. Remove from the oven and carefully transfer to a wire rack.

To make the compote, put the blackcurrants in a medium saucepan and add the honey. Bring to a low boil over a gentle heat, then simmer gently for a few minutes or until the juice is nice and thick and the berries have burst. Remove from the heat and leave to cool.

To assemble, place a scoop of the Coffee and Kahlúa Ice Cream in the middle dip of each pavlova, drizzle with the blackcurrant compote and sprinkle with the toasted chopped hazelnuts.

TIP It's the combination of flavours that works so well in this recipe, so if you don't have any coffee ice cream, use blackcurrant sorbet with coconut cream drizzled with Espresso Ripple (page 121).

CARAMELISED APPLE AND PECAN CHEESECAKE PIE

I was given this American recipe years ago and saved it, intending to make it one day because it sounded delicious. Fifteen years later I finally got round to adapting it and I'm so glad I did.

Serves: 10–12 **Equipment**: 23cm loose-bottomed flan tin; food processor (optional); electric hand mixer
Preparation time: 45 minutes plus minimum 4 hours chilling, or overnight **Cooking time:** Approx. 1 hour
Freeze: Yes – open freeze until solid, then wrap in foil and store in a rigid container in the freezer for up to 2 months

Base
175g dairy-, wheat- and gluten-free
   digestive biscuits
55g coconut butter or dairy-free
   block margarine
1 tsp ground cinnamon

Filling
75g dairy-free spread
90g unrefined soft light brown sugar
¼ tsp salt
1 tsp ground cinnamon
5 Granny Smith apples, peeled, cored
   and thinly sliced
100g pecans, toasted and chopped
225g dairy-free cream cheese,
   at room temperature
55g unrefined caster sugar
1 tsp vanilla extract
1 large egg, beaten
1 tbsp lemon juice

Caramel Sauce
150g unrefined soft light brown sugar
100g dairy-free spread
100ml single soya or almond cream
½ tsp vanilla extract
Pinch of sea salt

Topping
1 Granny Smith apple, peeled, cored
   and thinly sliced
15g unrefined soft light brown sugar
¼ tsp ground cinnamon

Put all the ingredients for the caramel sauce in a small heavy-based saucepan. Stirring constantly, bring to a gentle boil over a medium heat. Boil for a few minutes until it starts to look glossy, then cool.

Preheat the oven to 180°C/160°C fan/Gas 4 and lightly grease the base and sides of the flan tin.

Pulse the biscuits in a food processor until they resemble sand. Alternatively, put into a freezer bag and finely crush using a rolling pin.

Melt the coconut butter or margarine in a large heavy-based saucepan. Remove from the heat and stir in the biscuit crumbs and cinnamon. Firmly and evenly press the mixture into the base and sides of the flan tin. Bake in the preheated oven for 10 minutes, then set aside to cool.

For the filling, melt the dairy-free spread in a large frying pan over a medium heat. Add the brown sugar, salt and cinnamon and cook until just bubbling. Add the sliced apples and toss well to coat with the sugar syrup. Cook over a medium-high heat until the syrup has reduced and the apples are tender, 15–20 minutes. Set aside to cool.

Pour a layer of caramel sauce onto the biscuit base and sprinkle the chopped pecan nuts over the top. Chill in the fridge.

Beat the cream cheese using an electric hand mixer until smooth, then slowly beat in the caster sugar until combined. Add the vanilla, beaten egg and lemon juice and mix together until smooth.

Spoon the apples evenly over the caramel and pecan nuts. Spread the cream cheese filling over the apples. Place the apple for the topping on the cream cheese layer, then sprinkle with the sugar and cinnamon. Bake in the centre of the oven for 35–40 minutes or until a knife inserted in the centre comes out clean and the top has caramelised.

Leave to cool at room temperature, then chill for at least 4 hours, but preferably overnight. Slice with a sharp knife dipped in hot water.

BLUEBERRY CREAM CHEESE TART

The perfect summer tart; easy to make, beautiful to look at and delicious to eat.

Serves: 8–10 **Equipment:** 23cm tart tin; food processor (optional); electric hand mixer
Preparation time: 30 minutes plus minimum 1½ hours chilling **Cooking time:** Approx. 1 hour **Freeze:** No

---

Pastry
½ quantity Sweet Shortcrust Pastry
   (page 16)
1 egg, beaten with 1 tbsp soya, rice,
   almond or coconut milk

Filling
115g dairy-free cream cheese,
   at room temperature
60g dairy-free sour cream, at room
   temperature
60g unrefined caster sugar
Pinch of freshly grated nutmeg
Finely grated zest of 1 large lemon
3 large eggs, beaten
350g blueberries

TIP *For a much sharper-tasting
tart, replace the blueberries
with blackcurrants.*

Make the pastry, wrap in clingfilm and chill in the fridge for at least 1 hour, or overnight if possible.

Remove the chilled pastry from the fridge and place on a sheet of clingfilm lightly dusted with flour. Place another sheet of clingfilm over the top of the pastry and gently start to roll the pastry out into a rough circle 3mm thick. You might need to pull the clingfilm taut after several rolls to ensure it doesn't get caught up in the pastry. Remove the top sheet of clingfilm, then lift the bottom sheet up and turn over onto the tart tin. Gently press the pastry into place before peeling the clingfilm off. Trim the excess pastry by rolling the rolling pin across the top of the tin. Lightly prick the base with a fork and chill in the freezer for 30 minutes. Meanwhile, preheat the oven to 190°C/170°C fan/Gas 5 and place a baking sheet in the oven to heat.

Line the chilled pastry case with baking parchment and ceramic beans. Bake in the oven for 15 minutes or until the pastry starts to turn golden.

Remove from the oven and lift the parchment and ceramic beans out; take care, as they will be very hot. Brush the pastry with the beaten egg mixture and return to the oven for 10 minutes or until the pastry is a lovely golden colour. Set aside to cool, and increase the oven temperature to 220°C/200°C fan/Gas 7.

Using an electric hand mixer, beat the cream cheese and sour cream together, then beat in the sugar, nutmeg and lemon zest. Slowly beat in the eggs (over-beating at this stage will create lots of air bubbles that can cause cracking in the filling as it bakes).

Pour the mixture into the pastry case and sprinkle the blueberries over the surface.

Bake for 10 minutes, then reduce the oven temperature to 170°C/150°C fan/Gas 3 and bake for a further 20 minutes or until the filling is firm and golden. Remove from the oven and cool before serving.

LITTLE BLUEBERRY
AND VANILLA TRIFLES

We all lead busy lives, so it isn't always possible to spend as much time as we would like making meals from scratch, and although it isn't as straightforward for those of us with an allergy or intolerance, the choice of ingredients available today has greatly improved. These gorgeous little trifles are incredibly quick and easy to make, and while I usually have surplus cake somewhere in the house, there are occasions when I don't. In that case I am more than happy to use the 'free-from' supermarket muffins and ready-made dairy-free vanilla custard.

Serves: 6
Equipment: Six individual serving glasses or dishes; piping bag fitted with a nozzle (optional)
Preparation time: 30 minutes plus chilling
Freeze: No

1 quantity Coconut Cream
 (page 138)
250g blueberries, plus extra
 to decorate
25g unrefined caster sugar
2 tbsp crème de cassis
3 tbsp water
250g shop-bought 'free-from'
 muffins or gingerbread, Chocolate
 Genoise (page 101) or Lady's
 Fingers (page 152)
500g ready-made dairy-free
 vanilla custard
25g Honey-roasted Almonds
 (page 154), to serve

TIP *If making these trifles for children, substitute the crème de cassis for blackcurrant cordial.*

Make the Coconut Cream and chill in the fridge until needed.

Put all but a handful of the blueberries (reserve for the top) in a small saucepan with the sugar, cassis and water. Stir over a low heat for 5 minutes until the sugar has dissolved and the blueberries have started to burst.

Remove from the heat, cool and chill in the fridge for 30 minutes.

Chop your chosen muffins, gingerbread or sponge into small cubes and divide evenly between the serving glasses or dishes. Don't pack the pieces in too tightly as you need room for the blueberries, syrup and custard to slip down in between the cubes.

Spoon the blueberries into the glasses or dishes, making sure a few berries fall down between the cubes. Drizzle the blueberry syrup evenly over the berries, allowing it to soak into the cubes beneath.

Spoon the vanilla custard over the top of the berries.

Pipe or spoon the chilled Coconut Cream into swirls on top of the custard and decorate with a few reserved blueberries and a sprinkling of Honey-roasted Almonds.

CREME CARAMEL

As much as I love the heady flavour and fragrance of vanilla, it is equally nice on occasion to ring the changes, so when the mood takes me I replace the vanilla with the finely grated zest of 4 very large oranges.

Serves: 6
Equipment: Six 150ml ramekins or small heatproof bowls
Preparation time: 20 minutes plus minimum 2 hours chilling
Cooking time: 1¼ hours
Freeze: No

Custard
700ml coconut milk
1 vanilla pod, split lengthways
5 large eggs
75g unrefined caster sugar

Caramel
120g granulated sugar
2 tbsp water
A few drops of lemon juice

TIP *Don't worry if a thin skin forms over the custards when they cook; once you've removed them from the roasting tin, very gently run a small, sharp knife around the edge of the custard and peel the skin off, cover the custards and leave them to cool as directed.*

Put the milk in a small saucepan. Scrape out the seeds from the vanilla pod and add these to the milk with the pod. Bring to a gentle boil, then remove from the heat and leave to infuse.

Sprinkle the granulated sugar for the caramel evenly over the base of a small saucepan, then pour the water over the sugar, ensuring it is evenly moistened and there are no dry patches.

Place the pan over a low to medium heat until the sugar has dissolved into a clear syrup; don't be tempted to stir, as it could cause the sugar crystals to clump together. Add the lemon juice to help prevent the sugar from crystallising.

Continue cooking the caramel, swirling the pan very gently if the sugar starts to crystallise, but never stirring. Once the caramel has turned the colour of a new penny, remove from the heat.

Carefully pour the caramel into the base of the ramekins or small heatproof bowls and leave to harden for 15 minutes.

Preheat the oven to 150°C/130°C fan/Gas 2. Bring the milk back to the boil.

In a large bowl, lightly whisk the eggs and caster sugar together, then, whisking continuously, slowly pour in the hot milk. Strain the mixture through a nylon sieve set over a large jug to remove the vanilla and any small lumps.

Place the ramekins or bowls in a roasting tin and pour the custard into each one, over the hardened caramel.

Pour cold water into the tin to come about halfway up the ramekins or bowls, cover them with a sheet of baking parchment, then very carefully transfer the tin to the oven. Bake for 1 hour or until the custards are just set; if you give them a shake, they should tremble.

Carefully take the ramekins or bowls out of the tin, cover loosely and cool. Cover each cooled crème caramel with a piece of clingfilm so that it is touching the surface and chill in the fridge for at least 2 hours.

To serve, run a sharp knife around the edge of each crème caramel, place an individual shallow dish on top and invert; the caramel will gently pool around the custards.

COCONUT CREMA CATALANA

I had always thought of myself as a bit of a connoisseur of Crema Catalana, so I really wasn't convinced that a dairy-free version would be up to scratch. How wrong I was: whilst there is a very definite coconut flavour, the custard is still rich and creamy and the crisp shell still shatters satisfyingly – perfect.

Serves: 6
Equipment: Six 150ml ramekins or small heatproof bowls
Preparation time: 20 minutes plus overnight chilling
Cooking time: Approx. 1 hour
Freeze: No

Custard
3 large eggs plus 2 large yolks
50g unrefined caster sugar
570ml coconut cream
150ml coconut milk, chilled

Caramel
165g granulated sugar
115ml water
A few drops of lemon juice

TIP *I love a really thick layer of caramel over my custards, so don't worry if you find you have some left over. Leave the surplus in the saucepan to cool, then fill the pan with warm water to soak and the caramel will dissolve so that you can just tip it away.*

Preheat the oven to 170°C/150°C fan/Gas 3 and place the ramekins or bowls in a roasting tin.

Put the eggs and yolks and caster sugar into a large mixing bowl and lightly beat using a balloon whisk until nice and smooth.

Heat the coconut cream in a small saucepan until hand-hot, then gradually whisk it into the egg and sugar mixture. Once combined, stir in the chilled coconut milk.

Pour the mixture evenly into the ramekins or bowls, then pour boiling water into the roasting tin to come halfway up their sides. Very carefully transfer the roasting tin to the oven and bake for 35–40 minutes until the custard is lightly set and wobbles to the touch.

Remove the ramekins or bowls from the roasting tin, loosely cover and leave to cool. Cover the surface of each cooled custard with clingfilm and chill overnight in the fridge.

To make the caramel, sprinkle the granulated sugar evenly over the base of a small saucepan, then pour the water over the sugar, ensuring that it is evenly moistened and there are no dry patches.

Place over a low to medium heat until the sugar has dissolved into a clear syrup; don't be tempted to stir, as it could cause the sugar crystals to clump together. Add the lemon juice to help prevent the sugar from crystallising.

Continue cooking the caramel, swirling the pan very gently if the sugar starts to crystallise, but never stirring. Once the caramel has turned the colour of a new penny, remove from the heat.

Carefully pour the caramel over the surface of the chilled custards and leave to harden for 15 minutes before returning to the fridge for 1 hour to chill.

POTS AU CHOCOLAT WITH PRUNE AND ARMAGNAC CREAM

These little pots of chocolate mousse pack a seriously delicious punch and make the perfect supper party pud. Make them the day before your party, but remember to take them out of the fridge a few hours before you need them so that they can be served at room temperature.

Serves: 6 **Equipment:** Six 150ml ramekins or espresso cups; food processor or blender; electric hand mixer; piping bag fitted with a nozzle **Preparation time:** 30 minutes, including 20 minutes cooling **Cooking time:** 30–35 minutes **Freeze:** No

Pots au Chocolat

200g best-quality (60% cocoa) dark, dairy-free chocolate, chopped
500ml coconut cream
45g unrefined caster sugar
1 tsp espresso powder
Pinch of salt
6 large egg yolks
1 tsp vanilla extract

Prune and Armagnac Cream

100g Prunes Soaked in Armagnac (page 153 or see TIP on page 102)
6 tbsp hot water from the kettle
160ml coconut cream
½ tsp vanilla extract
2 tsp icing sugar

Preheat the oven to 180°C/160°C/Gas 4. Place the ramekins or espresso cups in a roasting tin.

Put the chocolate in a large heatproof bowl.

Heat the coconut cream, sugar, espresso powder and salt in a medium saucepan until hot and the sugar has dissolved; do not boil.

Pour the mixture over the chocolate, whisking with a balloon whisk until the chocolate has melted and the mixture is smooth. Leave to cool for about 20 minutes, then whisk in the egg yolks and vanilla extract.

To make it easier to pour, you can transfer the mixture to a large measuring jug at this point. Pour the mixture evenly into the ramekins or espresso cups.

Pour boiling water into the roasting tin so that it reaches halfway up the ramekins or espresso cups. Cover the tin tightly with foil and bake until the mousse is still slightly wobbly in the middle, 30–35 minutes.

Carefully remove from the oven and transfer the ramekins or espresso cups to a wire rack to cool to room temperature.

Put the Armagnac-soaked prunes into a food processor or blender and add the 6 tablespoons hot water; blitz to a smooth purée.

Put the coconut cream in a mixing bowl, add the vanilla extract and icing sugar and beat with an electric hand mixer until peaks are formed.

Carefully fold in the prune purée. I think it looks nicer in streaks rather than completely stirred in, so only cut through the cream with the spoon a couple of times before transferring to the piping bag. Pipe small swirls onto the cooled chocolate pots and serve slightly warm or at room temperature.

I DON'T THINK I HAVE EVER MET ANYONE
WHO DOESN'T LIKE ICE CREAM. CLOSE YOUR
EYES AND IMAGINE THE SHEER INDULGENCE
OF CREAMY VANILLA ICE CREAM SLOWLY
MELTING OVER STICKY TOFFEE PUDDINGS,
OR THE JOY OF A BLACKCURRANT SORBET
ON A WARM SUMMER'S DAY, OR A THICKLY
RIPPLED SCOOP OR TWO AT A CHILDREN'S
TEA PARTY... THERE REALLY IS NOTHING
QUITE LIKE HOMEMADE ICE CREAM. AND YES,
I DO LOVE SORBETS – EVEN LEMON ONES!

Ice Creams & Sorbets

MADAGASCAN VANILLA ICE CREAM

Prior to giving up dairy I wasn't a massive ice cream fan, but of course once I couldn't have it I became obsessed. This was the first recipe I made with my newly purchased ice cream machine and I was so excited that I didn't read the instructions properly and poured the custard into the bowl before starting the beater; yup, you guessed it, the custard froze to the sides in a horrible mess and I ended up in floods of tears. I rallied and tried again, and I'm so pleased I did. Proper vanilla ice cream is a complete revelation and so adaptable; I serve mine drizzled and rippled with some of my favourite toppings, or alongside summer tarts and warm winter puddings.

Makes: Approx. 625ml
Equipment: Ice cream machine
Preparation time: Approx. 30 minutes
Cooking time: 15 minutes
Cooling time: Thoroughly chilled custard will spend less time churning in the machine and the shorter the churning, the smaller the ice crystals and the smoother the ice cream. So cool for approx. 90 minutes, and then a minimum 8 hours or overnight chilling
Freeze: Minimum of 5–6 hours then transfer to fridge for 20 minutes before serving. Homemade ice cream should be eaten within 1 week

500ml soya, almond, rice or coconut milk
75g unrefined caster sugar
Pinch of salt
1 vanilla pod, split lengthways
6 large egg yolks
45g dried almond milk powder
2 tbsp sunflower oil
½ tsp vanilla extract

Put the milk, sugar and salt into a medium saucepan.

Scrape out the seeds from the vanilla pod and add to the milk along with the pod.

Warm the mixture over a medium heat until the sugar has dissolved.

In a large mixing bowl, whisk the egg yolks, almond powder and sunflower oil until you have a thick, smooth paste.

Gradually pour about one third of the warmed milk onto the egg yolk mixture, whisking continuously. Return the mixture to the saucepan and cook over a gentle heat, stirring constantly with a wooden spoon and making sure it doesn't boil.

When the custard has thickened and coats the back of the spoon, strain through a metal sieve into a clean bowl, remove the vanilla pod and stir in the vanilla extract.

To cool the mixture, set the bowl in a larger bowl filled with ice and stir the mixture occasionally to prevent a skin from forming. This could take up to 90 minutes, depending on room temperature.

Chill the cooled mixture in the fridge for at least 8 hours, or preferably overnight.

Remove the chilled custard from the fridge and churn in the ice cream machine according to the manufacturer's instructions.

Transfer the soft-scoop ice cream to a suitable container and place in the freezer until ready to serve. Vanilla ice cream tastes amazing drizzled with a little Butterscotch Sauce.

TIP *Don't throw your vanilla pod away; rinse and dry it thoroughly, then bury it in a jar of caster sugar – vanilla sugar is delicious and can be used in lots of cake recipes and sprinkled over sponges.*

RICH CHOCOLATE ICE CREAM

Really and truly this recipe should be called 'rich chocolate gelato' because it doesn't contain cream, but I'm not a great one for splitting hairs and as far as I'm concerned it is rich, smooth, dark and delicious – just like a really good ice cream should be. For a very special treat I love to serve a couple of scoops with my Prunes Soaked in Armagnac (page 153), a spoonful of lightly whipped coconut cream and a drizzle of the prune liquor.

Makes: Approx. 750ml
Equipment: Ice cream machine
Preparation time: Approx. 30 minutes
Cooking time: 15 minutes
Cooling time: Thoroughly chilled custard will spend less time churning in the machine and the shorter the churning, the smaller the ice crystals and the smoother the ice cream. So cool for approx. 90 minutes, and then a minimum 8 hours or overnight chilling
Freeze: Minimum of 5–6 hours then transfer to fridge for 20 minutes before serving. Homemade ice cream should be eaten within 1 week

50g cocoa powder
500ml soya, almond, rice or coconut milk
Pinch of salt
140g best-quality (60% cocoa) dark, dairy-free chocolate, chopped (or drops)
150g unrefined caster sugar
4 large egg yolks
45g soya or almond powder
2 tbsp sunflower oil

In a medium saucepan, whisk together the cocoa powder, half the milk and the salt. Slowly bring to the boil.

Put the chocolate in a large heatproof bowl and pour the boiling milk over, stirring until the chocolate has melted.

Using the same saucepan, warm the remaining 250ml milk with the sugar, stirring until the sugar dissolves.

In another bowl, whisk the egg yolks, soya or almond milk powder and sunflower oil together; the mixture will be a bit lumpy, but this is fine.

Add some of the warm milk and sugar mixture to the egg yolks, whisking until all the lumps are dissolved. Any small ones remaining will soon disappear over the heat.

Pour the mixture back into the milk left in the saucepan and cook over a low heat, whisking constantly and scraping the bottom of the pan; don't let it boil.

Once the custard is thick enough to coat the back of a spoon, remove from the heat and strain through a metal sieve into the chocolate mixture. Stir until smooth. If the chocolate mixture seems a little lumpy, just strain it again.

To cool the mixture, set the bowl in a larger bowl filled with ice and stir the mixture occasionally to prevent a skin from forming. This could take up to 90 minutes, depending on room temperature.

Chill the cooled mixture in the fridge for at least 8 hours, or preferably overnight.

Remove the chilled chocolate custard from the fridge and churn in the ice cream machine according to the manufacturer's instructions.

Transfer the soft-scoop ice cream to a suitable container and place in the freezer until ready to serve.

TIP *Add ½ teaspoon chilli sauce to the melted chocolate to give the ice cream a bit of warmth; don't be tempted to add more than this, as you should taste the chocolate first, with a hit of chilli arriving after.*

COFFEE AND KAHLUA ICE CREAM WITH MOCHA AND ESPRESSO RIPPLE

As a child I can remember always being disappointed by the amount of ripple in my raspberry ripple ice cream, so when I started making my own ice creams, I vowed I would always swirl as much ripple through them as I decently could, and this one is no exception.

Makes: Approx. 750ml **Equipment:** Ice cream machine **Preparation time:** Approx. 30 minutes
Cooking time: 15 minutes **Cooling time:** Thoroughly chilled custard will spend less time churning in the machine and the shorter the churning, the smaller the ice crystals and the smoother the ice cream. So cool for approx. 90 minutes, and then a minimum 8 hours or overnight chilling **Freeze:** Minimum of 5–6 hours then transfer to fridge for 20 minutes before serving. Homemade ice cream should be eaten within 1 week

---

500ml coconut cream
250ml coconut milk
75g unrefined granulated sugar
3 large egg yolks
2 tbsp espresso powder
Pinch of salt
50ml Kahlúa or coffee liqueur

Espresso Ripple
40g unrefined granulated sugar
20ml agave nectar
2 tsp espresso powder
65ml water
25g cocoa powder

First make the espresso ripple by whisking all the ingredients together in a small saucepan and heating until it starts to bubble. Gently simmer for 4–5 minutes or until thick and syrupy. Remove from the heat, leave to cool, then chill in the fridge until required.

To make the ice cream, put the coconut cream, milk and sugar into a saucepan and gently bring to the boil. Remove from the heat and leave to cool for a few minutes.

Whisk the egg yolks, espresso powder and salt together in a heatproof bowl until combined, then, stirring constantly, slowly pour the cream mixture onto the eggs. When combined, pour the mixture back into the saucepan and gently heat until just below boiling point. Remove from the heat.

To cool the mixture, pour into a bowl, then set the bowl in a larger bowl filled with ice, stirring occasionally to prevent the mixture from splitting. This could take up to 90 minutes, depending on room temperature.

Chill the coffee custard mixture in the fridge for at least 8 hours or preferably overnight.

Remove the chilled custard from the fridge. If it has split, give it a really good stir, then add the Kahlúa and churn the custard in the ice cream machine according to the manufacturer's instructions.

Pour the soft-scoop ice cream into a suitable freezer container and drizzle the espresso ripple over the surface, using a round-ended knife to swirl the ripple through the ice cream. Freeze until needed. Serve with a sprinkling of crushed Peanut Brittle (page 155) for added crunch.

PEANUT BUTTER AND RASPBERRY RIPPLE ICE CREAM

As you can imagine, this American classic is a real hit with my son Charlie and his chums. I use a very good-quality peanut butter without added sugar and then swirl tonnes of raspberry ripple through it; not only does it taste yummy but it looks pretty amazing as well.

Makes: Approx. 1 litre
Equipment: Ice cream machine
Preparation time: Approx. 30 minutes
Cooling time: Thoroughly chilled custard will spend less time churning in the machine and the shorter the churning, the smaller the ice crystals and the smoother the ice cream. So cool for approx. 90 minutes, and then a minimum 8 hours or overnight chilling
Freeze: Minimum of 5–6 hours then transfer to fridge for 20 minutes before serving. Homemade ice cream should be eaten within 1 week

235ml coconut milk
470ml coconut cream
195g crunchy peanut butter
115g unrefined soft light
   brown sugar
1 tbsp vanilla extract
200g Raspberry Ripple (page 149)

Put the coconut milk, coconut cream, peanut butter and sugar into a medium saucepan over a low heat. Bring to the boil, stirring occasionally to make sure the sugar dissolves.

Remove from the heat and stir in the vanilla extract. Transfer the mixture to a large bowl, cover the surface with clingfilm to prevent a skin from forming and chill in the fridge for a minimum of 8 hours, but preferably overnight.

Whilst the ice cream is chilling, put the Raspberry Ripple in the fridge to cool too.

Remove the chilled ice cream from the fridge, give it a quick whisk to loosen it, then churn it in the ice cream machine according to the manufacturer's instructions.

Transfer the soft-scoop ice cream to a suitable container and dribble the Raspberry Ripple over the surface. Using a round-ended knife, swirl the ripple through the ice cream.

Place the ice cream in the freezer until ready to serve.

LEMON CUSTARD GELATO WITH HOT LEMON SAUCE

Having spent years being offered lemon sorbets as a consolation prize – most restaurants still don't offer a proper dairy-free pudding – I was determined to find a lemon ice cream recipe that was so special I would actually choose to eat it. This is it, the most fabulous lemon gelato you will ever have, and the hot sauce isn't bad either!

Makes: Approx. 1.5 litres
Equipment: Ice cream machine
Preparation time: Approx. 30 minutes
Cooking time: 15 minutes
Cooling time: Thoroughly chilled custard will spend less time churning in the machine and the shorter the churning, the smaller the ice crystals and the smoother the ice cream. So cool for approx. 90 minutes, and then a minimum 8 hours or overnight chilling
Freeze: Minimum of 5–6 hours then transfer to fridge for 20 minutes before serving. Homemade ice cream should be eaten within 1 week

6 large egg yolks
30g soya powder
2 tbsp sunflower oil
200g unrefined caster sugar
500ml soya cream
250ml soya milk
Grated zest of 2 lemons
185ml lemon juice (6–8 lemons)
Pinch of salt

Hot Lemon Sauce
1 heaped tsp cornflour
Juice and grated zest of 2 lemons
50g unrefined caster sugar

In a large mixing bowl, whisk together the egg yolks, soya powder and sunflower oil until you have a nice, thick, smooth paste.

Transfer the mixture to a medium saucepan and whisk together with the sugar until well combined.

Slowly whisk in the soya cream and milk until completely incorporated.

Cook over a gentle heat, stirring constantly with a wooden spoon, without letting it boil. When the custard has thickened and coats the back of the spoon, remove from the heat and strain through a metal sieve into a clean bowl.

Stir in the lemon zest, lemon juice and salt, cover and chill in the fridge overnight.

Remove the custard from the fridge and strain through a metal sieve to remove the lemon zest. Churn in the ice cream machine according to manufacturer's instructions.

Transfer the soft-scoop ice cream to a suitable container and place in the freezer until ready to serve.

To make the hot lemon sauce, mix the cornflour with 2 tablespoons of the lemon juice in a heatproof bowl.

Put the remaining lemon juice and the sugar in a small saucepan and place over a low heat until the sugar has dissolved. Add the zest and bring to simmering point, but do not boil.

Pour the liquid over the cornflour and lemon mixture, stirring well. Return to the saucepan and cook over a low heat, stirring until the sauce begins to thicken, a further 2 minutes.

Leave to cool slightly before pouring over the gelato to serve.

TIP *To give the hot sauce a bit of a kick, add 2 tablespoons ginger syrup from a jar of stem ginger to the sugar and lemon juice.*

BROWN BREAD ICE CREAM

Brown bread ice cream had always fascinated me, but for some reason I just never got round to trying it, probably because it wasn't available in the local supermarket and the thought of making my own just never entered my head. So once I had mastered vanilla ice cream, this was the recipe I tackled next. I love the inclusion of the Grand Marnier, but it tastes just as good without it.

Makes: Approx. 625ml
Equipment: Ice cream machine
Preparation time: Approx. 30 minutes
Cooking time: 15 minutes
Cooling time: Thoroughly chilled custard will spend less time churning in the machine and the shorter the churning, the smaller the ice crystals and the smoother the ice cream. So cool for approx. 90 minutes, and then a minimum 8 hours or overnight chilling
Freeze: Minimum of 5–6 hours then transfer to fridge for 20 minutes before serving. Homemade ice cream should be eaten within 1 week

1 quantity Madagascan Vanilla Ice Cream (page 118), without vanilla extract

1 tbsp Grand Marnier or good-quality brandy

40g dairy-free spread, plus extra for greasing

50g light muscovado sugar

80g brown wheat- and gluten-free breadcrumbs (don't use crusts)

Make the Madagascan Vanilla Ice Cream up to the stage where you strain the thickened custard into a bowl, stirring the Grand Marnier or brandy into the strained mixture. Chill as directed.

When the custard is chilled, preheat the oven to 180°C/160°C fan/Gas 4.

Melt the dairy-free spread in a heavy-based saucepan.

Remove from the heat, add the sugar and stir until combined.

Add the breadcrumbs and stir well until they are evenly coated in the sugar mixture.

Spread the breadcrumbs out on a lightly greased baking tray and transfer to the oven, turning them frequently until they are browned and nicely crisp, about 15 minutes. Set aside to cool.

Rub the cooled breadcrumbs between your fingers to break up any stubborn clumps.

Remove the chilled custard from the fridge and churn according to the manufacturer's instructions. Five minutes before the end of churning, add the breadcrumbs to the ice cream and continue churning until they are thoroughly mixed in.

Transfer the soft-scoop ice cream to a suitable container and place in the freezer until ready to serve.

WHITE CHOCOLATE AND TOASTED HAZELNUT ICE CREAM

A lot of people turn their noses up at white chocolate, snobbishly claiming it isn't really chocolate at all. This might be true, but I have always loved it, and as a child I frequently chose a white chocolate bar over other bars when I had pocket money to spend. Dairy-free white chocolate is notoriously difficult to work with, so you can imagine my delight when I discovered I could buy dairy-free white couverture powder. It is incredibly easy to use and perfect for recipes that call for melted white chocolate. I serve this ice cream with fruit pies, crumbles and sponge puddings.

Makes: Approx. 1 litre
Equipment: Ice cream machine; electric hand mixer
Preparation time: Approx. 30 minutes
Cooking time: 6–8 minutes
Cooling time: Thoroughly chilled custard will spend less time churning in the machine and the shorter the churning, the smaller the ice crystals and the smoother the ice cream. So cool for approx. 90 minutes, and then a minimum 8 hours or overnight chilling
Freeze: Minimum of 5–6 hours then transfer to fridge for 20 minutes before serving. Homemade ice cream should be eaten within 1 week

100g white couverture powder
30g dried soya or almond milk powder
1 tbsp sunflower oil
150ml soya cream
650ml soya milk
1 vanilla pod, split lengthways
1 large egg white
150g unrefined caster sugar
50g blanched hazelnuts
½ tsp sea salt

Put the couverture powder in a medium heatproof bowl.

Mix the soya or almond powder, sunflower oil and soya cream together in another medium bowl until combined.

Gently heat the milk in a medium saucepan until it reaches a simmer, then remove from the heat and whisk into the soya or almond powder and cream mixture.

Return the mixture to the pan and bring to the boil, then remove from the heat and pour onto the couverture powder, whisking with a balloon whisk until smooth.

Add the split vanilla pod to the mixture and chill in the fridge for 30 minutes.

While the custard is cooling, preheat the oven to 180°C/160°C fan/Gas 4. Spread the hazelnuts out evenly on a baking tray, sprinkle with the sea salt and toast in the oven for 6–8 minutes until starting to brown. Tip onto a board to cool for 10 minutes, then roughly chop.

In a large mixing bowl, and using an electric hand mixer, whisk together the egg white and sugar to a soft peak meringue.

Remove the chilled mixture from the fridge, remove the vanilla pod and gently pour into the meringue mixture. Whisk for 30 seconds to combine.

Cover with clingfilm and return to the fridge to chill for at least 8 hours but preferably overnight.

Remove the chilled custard from the fridge and churn in the ice cream machine according to the manufacturer's instructions.

Add the chopped hazelnuts to the ice cream 5 minutes before the end of churning. Transfer the soft-scoop ice cream to a suitable container and place in the freezer until ready to serve.

MERLOT GELATO

I know I grumble about always being offered sorbet, but when a good friend of mine served this recipe at a summer supper a few years ago, I certainly didn't complain. Whether you call it sorbet or gelato, it is without doubt incredibly grown up, absolutely delicious and the perfect dessert for a warm summer evening; on that occasion I definitely had more than one scoop!

Makes: Approx. 1.2 litres
Equipment: Ice cream machine
Preparation time: 1 hour
Cooling time: Thoroughly chilled mixture will spend less time churning in the machine and the shorter the churning, the smaller the ice crystals and the smoother the ice cream. So cool for approx. 90 minutes, and then a minimum 8 hours or overnight chilling
Freeze: Minimum of 5–6 hours then transfer to fridge for 20 minutes before serving. Homemade sorbets and gelato should be eaten within 1 week

350ml Merlot or Beaujolais wine
350ml water
225ml orange juice (approx. 4 large oranges)
Juice of 1 lemon
175ml agave nectar
350g fresh or frozen raspberries
1 tbsp crème de cassis (optional)
1 tsp vanilla extract

Put the wine, water, orange and lemon juice and agave nectar into a large saucepan and bring to the boil, stirring occasionally.

Remove from the heat and add the raspberries, crème de cassis, if using, and vanilla extract. Cover and leave to stand for 1 hour.

Carefully strain through a fine nylon sieve into a large bowl to remove the raspberry pips. Use a wooden spoon to firmly press the berries through, leaving just the pips behind.

Cover the bowl with clingfilm and chill for at least 8 hours, but preferably overnight.

Remove the chilled liquid from the fridge and churn in the ice cream machine according to the manufacturer's instructions.

Spoon the churned gelato into a suitable container and freeze for a minimum of 2 hours.

Serve with a handful of fresh berries and a sprig of mint.

WALNUT PRALINE ICE CREAM

This is a delicately flavoured ice cream with a wonderfully nutty crunch, absolutely perfect served with apple pie.

Makes: Approx. 750ml
Equipment: Electric hand mixer
Preparation time: Approx.
1 hour
Cooking time: 5 minutes
Cooling time: Overnight
chilling
Freeze: Minimum of 5–6
hours then transfer to fridge
for 20 minutes before serving.
Homemade ice cream should be
eaten within 1 week

100g walnut halves
3 x 400ml cans coconut milk, chilled
1½ tsp vanilla extract
1½ tbsp icing sugar
100g unrefined caster sugar
50ml water
2 large egg yolks

Walnut Praline
100g walnut halves
100g granulated sugar
50ml water
A few drops of freshly squeezed
    lemon juice
Pinch of salt

Preheat the oven to 170°C/150°C fan/Gas 3. Spread all the walnuts (for the ice cream and the praline) out evenly on a baking tray lined with baking parchment. Lightly toast in the oven for 5 minutes or until you can just begin to smell them; you just want to bring the oils out. Tip onto a board to cool for a few minutes, then roughly chop half and set the remaining half aside (for the praline).

Turn the chilled cans of coconut milk upside down, open and drain the liquid out. Spoon the remaining cream (500ml in total) into a large bowl, add the vanilla and icing sugar, then beat using an electric hand mixer to just combine. Add the chopped nuts and refrigerate overnight.

To make the praline, sprinkle the sugar evenly over the base of a saucepan, then pour the water over it, ensuring it is evenly moistened and there are no dry patches. Place over a low to medium heat, without stirring, until the sugar has dissolved into a clear syrup. Add the lemon juice to prevent the sugar from crystallising. Stir in the salt.

Continue cooking the caramel, gently and without turning the heat up. Once the caramel is the colour of a new penny, remove from the heat and, working very quickly, add the reserved walnut halves and stir so that they are all covered. Tip onto a baking sheet, spread into a single layer and leave to cool.

Use a sharp knife to break the cooled praline into small pieces, then store overnight in an airtight container in the freezer.

Next day, strain the chilled coconut cream mixture through a metal sieve into a large bowl to remove the walnuts. If the cream has firmed up, use the back of a wooden spoon to push it through the sieve. Discard the nuts, whip the cream with the electric hand mixer into soft peaks and set aside.

Heat the sugar and water in small saucepan, stirring until the sugar has dissolved. Cook the syrup for 3 minutes without stirring.

Meanwhile, put the egg yolks in a bowl and whisk with the electric hand mixer until they begin to turn light and fluffy. Pour the syrup into the yolks, whisking continuously until pale and very fluffy. Fold in the whipped coconut cream until just combined, sprinkle the praline over the mixture and fold it in, then pour the mixture into a suitable freezer container and freeze. Remove from the freezer about 20 minutes before serving.

CHRISTMAS PUDDING ICE CREAM

I think it's a given that there will always be Christmas pudding leftovers, and whilst I love slicing mine up and frying it with a little honey, this amazingly easy ice cream recipe is a huge hit with the younger members of my family, especially when served up in a wheat- and gluten-free waffle cornet with a festive Christmas sparkler on top!

Makes: Approx. 600ml
Equipment: Food processor; ice cream machine
Preparation time: Approx. 30 minutes
Cooling time: Thoroughly chilled custard will spend less time churning in the machine and the shorter the churning, the smaller the ice crystals and the smoother the ice cream. So cool for approx. 90 minutes, and then a minimum 8 hours or overnight chilling
Freeze: Minimum of 5–6 hours then transfer to fridge for 20 minutes before serving. Homemade ice cream should be eaten within 1 week

500ml coconut milk
50g unrefined caster sugar
4 large egg yolks
2 tbsp rum
175g leftover Christmas pudding
75g coconut cream

Put the milk and sugar into a medium saucepan and bring to the boil, then remove from the heat and leave to cool for a few minutes.

Whisk the egg yolks in a mixing bowl, then, stirring constantly, slowly pour the milk onto the eggs. When combined, pour the mixture back into the saucepan and gently heat until just below boiling point; don't worry if the custard looks as though it has split.

Remove from the heat and stir in the rum.

Put the Christmas pudding into a food processor, add a ladleful of the custard and blend to a smooth paste. Transfer to a bowl, add the remaining custard and stir until combined.

Leave to cool, then cover and chill in the fridge for at least 8 hours or overnight.

Whip the coconut cream to soft peaks and fold into the chilled custard, then churn in the ice cream machine according to the manufacturer's instructions.

Transfer the soft-scoop ice cream to a suitable container and place in the freezer until ready to serve.

BANANA AND COCONUT ICE CREAM

This has to be one of the easiest and creamiest ice creams I make, and is a brilliant way of using up those leftover ripe bananas: just chop them into bite-sized pieces and freeze in a freezer bag; they are also great added to smoothies.

Makes: Approx. 750ml
Equipment: Food processor; ice cream machine
Preparation time: Approx. 15 minutes
Cooling time: 2 hours
Freeze: Minimum of 5–6 hours then transfer to fridge for 20 minutes before serving. Homemade ice cream should be eaten within 1 week

3½ large bananas, frozen
400ml can coconut milk
70g coconut palm sugar
1 tbsp dark rum
1 tsp vanilla extract

Put all the ingredients into a food processor and blend until completely smooth.

Cover and chill in the fridge for 2 hours.

Remove from the fridge and churn in the ice cream machine according to the manufacturer's instructions.

Pour the soft-scoop ice cream into a suitable container and freeze. Remove from the freezer about 30 minutes before needed.

Serve with either Dark and Delicious Chocolate Syrup (page 138) or a drizzle of Espresso Ripple (page 121).

CHOCOLATE SORBET

Whilst I like chocolate ice cream very much, I really lurrrrrve chocolate sorbet. It is rich, dark and smooth, and there's no creaminess to get in the way of that gorgeous cocoa hit. Serve with a scoop of Blackcurrant Sorbet (page 134) and a sprig of mint, for the perfect after-dinner treat.

Makes: Approx. 1 litre
Equipment: Ice cream machine
Preparation time: Approx. 30 minutes
Cooling time: Minimum 8 hours or overnight chilling
Freeze: Minimum of 5–6 hours then transfer to fridge for 20 minutes before serving. Homemade sorbet should be eaten within 1 week

550ml water
80g cocoa powder
200g unrefined caster sugar
170g best-quality (60% cocoa) dark, dairy-free chocolate, very finely chopped
½ tsp vanilla extract
¼ tsp salt

Whisk the water, cocoa powder and sugar together in a medium saucepan, then bring to the boil over a medium heat, stirring the mixture continuously.

Remove from the heat and add the chopped chocolate. Leave to rest for 30 seconds, then add the vanilla extract and salt. Stir until the chocolate has completely melted.

Leave to cool completely, then cover the surface with clingfilm and chill in the fridge for at least 8 hours or preferably overnight.

Remove the sorbet from the fridge, give it a quick whisk, then churn in the ice cream machine according to the manufacturer's instructions.

Pour the sorbet into a suitable container and freeze. Transfer to the fridge 20 minutes before serving and enjoy.

BLACKCURRANT SORBET AND MINT SHORTBREAD SANDWICH

To my son Charlie and me, blackcurrant sorbet means only one thing: summer hols in Salcombe, Devon. It's become a family tradition that at the end of each day we are dropped off at the bottom of Fore Street, where we treat ourselves to the most delicious blackcurrant sorbet from the Salcombe Dairy, before slowly wending our way home. My mint shortbread complements the intensely tart sorbet perfectly, and as Charlie would say: lush!

Makes: Approx. 1 litre sorbet and 12 biscuits
Equipment: Ice cream machine; 20cm square cake tin; 8cm square, round or rectangular cookie cutter
Preparation time: Approx. 30 minutes
Cooking time: 1¼ hours
Cooling time: Minimum 8 hours or overnight chilling
Freeze: Minimum of 5–6 hours then transfer to fridge for 20 minutes before serving. Homemade sorbet should be eaten within 1 week

Blackcurrant Sorbet

400g blackcurrants, fresh or frozen
125ml runny honey
60g unrefined caster sugar
500ml water
Grated zest and juice of 1 big lemon

Mint Shortbread

175g dairy-free spread
75g unrefined caster sugar, plus an extra 1 tbsp for sprinkling
1 tbsp finely chopped fresh mint
175g wheat- and gluten-free plain flour, plus extra for dusting
1 tsp xanthan gum
75g fine polenta

Put all the sorbet ingredients into a large saucepan and bring to a quick boil, then reduce the heat and simmer for 10 minutes.

Strain the fruit in small batches through a nylon sieve into a bowl, pressing the fruit hard with the back of a spoon to ensure you squeeze all the flesh and juice through, leaving the pips and skin behind.

Cover the bowl with clingfilm and chill for a minimum of 8 hours but preferably overnight.

Churn the chilled mixture in the ice cream machine according to the manufacturer's instructions.

Whilst the sorbet is churning, line the cake tin with clingfilm, ensuring you have a minimum of 5cm overlap on 2 ends (to help lift it out). Spoon the churned sorbet into the lined tin, cover with clingfilm and freeze for at least 5–6 hours.

To make the biscuits, preheat the oven to 150°C/130°C fan/Gas 2 and line a baking sheet with baking parchment.

Put the dairy-free spread into a large bowl and, using a wooden spoon, beat until nice and soft. Add the 75g caster sugar and chopped mint and beat until combined.

Sift in the flour and xanthan gum and add the polenta. Stir to combine, then, using your hands, bring the dough together; it will be soft and slightly sticky.

Roll out the dough to a 3mm thickness between 2 pieces of clingfilm lightly dusted with flour. Stamp out biscuits using the cookie cutter and carefully transfer to the lined baking sheet.

Bake for 1 hour or until golden, then remove from the oven, cool for 5 minutes and sprinkle with the tablespoon of caster sugar. Transfer to a wire rack to cool completely.

When ready to serve, lift the sorbet out of the tin and onto a board and, using the same cutter you used to make the biscuits, carefully stamp out a piece of sorbet and sandwich between 2 mint biscuits.

Creams & Sauces

A LITTLE OF WHAT YOU FANCY IS GOOD
FOR YOU – OR SO I'M RELIABLY INFORMED
– SO ADD A SWIRL OF COCONUT CREAM,
A RIPPLE OR TWO OF CARAMEL AND
CHOCOLATE, A SPRINKLING OF HONEY-
ROASTED NUTS OR A SCATTERING OF
PEANUT BRITTLE, AND TURN A SPECIAL
TREAT INTO SOMETHING EXTRAORDINARY.

DARK AND DELICIOUS CHOCOLATE SYRUP

Divinely rich, this is perfect for drizzling over ice creams, cheesecakes and pancakes or stirring into milk for a delicious shake. Be warned, a little goes a very long way!

Makes: 500ml
Preparation time: 5 minutes
Cooking time: 15 minutes
Freeze: Yes – cool completely and freeze in an airtight container or ziplock freezer bag for up to 2 months. Defrost overnight in the fridge.

75g cocoa powder
100g unrefined caster sugar
80g agave nectar
250ml water
¼ tsp vanilla extract
60g best-quality (60%) dark, dairy-free chocolate, roughly chopped (or use drops)

Whisk the cocoa powder, sugar, agave nectar and water together in a heavy-based saucepan and heat gently over a medium heat until the cocoa has dissolved, then bring to a gentle boil.

Once the syrup is boiling, remove from the heat and stir in the vanilla extract. Add the chocolate, whisking until it has melted and the syrup is smooth and glossy.

Leave to cool slightly, then transfer to a sterilised bottle or jar (see page 144) and store in the fridge for up to 2 weeks. Gently reheat before use, or serve at room temperature.

TIP *I make my chocolate syrup a few days before I need it, which allows time for the syrup to thicken and the chocolate flavour to deepen.*

COCONUT CREAM

You need to use full-fat canned coconut milk or coconut cream for this, as light milk just won't work. Also, certain brands do not whip successfully into peaks – the cream will still taste delicious and can be used in place of double cream, but it won't hold its shape. (See page 9 for advice on the best brands to use.) Because the milk needs to be cold for whipping and have time to separate, I always keep several cans in the fridge. I add a small amount of icing sugar and vanilla, but you can add more or less depending on personal taste.

Makes: Will vary depending on the fat content of individual can
Equipment: Electric hand mixer
Preparation time: 5 minutes
Freeze: No

400ml can full-fat coconut milk, chilled
½ tsp vanilla extract
½ tbsp icing sugar

Carefully turn the chilled can upside down, open and drain the liquid out. Spoon the remaining cream into a large bowl, add the vanilla extract and icing sugar, then beat with an electric hand mixer until soft peaks form; don't over-beat or the cream will become dry and grainy.

Chill the cream in the fridge until needed, as it will continue to thicken the colder it gets.

TIP *To ring the changes, ripple fruit coulis (pages 142–3) or chocolate sauce through the cream just before serving.*

RICH AND CREAMY VANILLA CUSTARD OR CREME ANGLAISE

Yes, you can buy very nice dairy-free custard in the supermarket, but really and truly, nothing beats a freshly homemade one. You can choose the milk you use, it is simple and quick to make and you can add different flavours to turn it into a very grown-up custard indeed!

Makes: Approx. 340ml and serves 6
Preparation time: 5 minutes
Cooking time: 10 minutes
Freeze: No

300ml soya, rice, almond or
  coconut milk
½ vanilla pod, split lengthways
4 large egg yolks
40g unrefined caster sugar

Put the milk into a medium saucepan, scrape out the seeds from the vanilla pod and add them and the pod to the milk. Gently heat until nicely warm, then remove from the heat.

In a medium heatproof bowl, lightly whisk the egg yolks and sugar together, then strain the warmed milk into them (discard the vanilla pod, or see TIP on page 118) and keep whisking before returning to the saucepan.

Cook over a low heat until lightly thickened, without letting it boil. Give a final whisk and pour into a serving jug.

CUSTARD VARIATIONS

Grand Marnier
Add 2 tablespoons Grand Marnier to the finished custard; give a quick whisk to combine before serving. Delicious with a Chunky Marmalade Sponge (page 78) or poured into a cracked Orange and Grand Marnier Soufflé (page 68).

Coffee
Whisk 2 teaspoons espresso powder into the milk just before heating. Increase the quantity of espresso powder if you like a really strong coffee flavour. Delicious served with Warm and Gooey Chocolate Fondant Puddings (page 64).

Cinnamon
Omit the vanilla and add 4–6 crushed cinnamon sticks to the milk before heating, then leave to infuse for 30 minutes. Strain before adding the milk to the egg yolks.

Citrus
Omit the vanilla and add the finely grated zest of 3 large lemons to the milk just before heating. After heating, leave to infuse for 30 minutes, then strain out the zest before adding the milk to the egg yolks and sugar.

BLACKCURRANT RIPPLE

My absolute favourite fruity flavour, blackcurrants are such an intense taste sensation that you only need a quick swirl through ice cream or a thick smear on sponge to remind you of warm summer days and holidays by the sea. I use frozen blackcurrants in this recipe because preparing them can be very time-consuming and of course you can only buy them in the summer months. A store of prepared and frozen blackcurrants makes life a lot easier and will provide you with your very own winter rescue remedy!

Makes: Approx. 400 ml
Cooking time: 35–45 minutes
Freeze: No – store in the fridge for up to 1 week

400g frozen blackcurrants
200g unrefined granulated sugar, or to taste
25ml lemon juice (approx. ½ lemon)
150ml water

Put the blackcurrants, sugar, lemon juice and water into a saucepan and slowly bring to the boil, stirring regularly to stop the sugar burning.

Reduce to a slowly bubbling simmer until the blackcurrants start to fall apart, about 10 minutes. If you prefer your syrups sweet rather than tart, add a little more sugar at this stage.

Remove the pan from the heat and strain the fruit through a metal sieve into a bowl, pressing the fruit really hard with the back of a spoon to ensure you have all the flesh and juice squeezed through.

Return the juice to the pan and bring to a slowly bubbling simmer. It should become thick and syrupy, which could take 25–35 minutes.

Remove from the heat and leave to cool completely; the ripple will thicken as it cools. Store in a sterilised jar (see page 144) in the fridge for up to 7 days.

BLACKCURRANT COULIS

Perfect drizzled over ice cream, served with cheesecakes or layered in trifles.

Makes: Approx. 150ml
Preparation time: 15 minutes
Freeze: Yes – freeze in small batches for up to 6 months and defrost at room temperature

250g fresh blackcurrants, or frozen and defrosted
50g unrefined caster sugar
100ml water
½ tsp vanilla extract

Put the blackcurrants, sugar and water into a small saucepan, slowly bring to the boil and then simmer for 5 minutes.

Remove from the heat and add the vanilla extract, then leave to cool for 5 minutes.

Strain the fruit in small batches through a nylon sieve placed over a bowl. Press the fruit very hard with the back of a spoon to ensure you have all the flesh and juice squeezed through, leaving behind just the pips and skin.

Taste and add extra sugar, if preferred.

Serve chilled or at room temperature. Store in a sterilised jar in the fridge for up to 7 days.

RASPBERRY COULIS

I can't think of many chocolate or lemon puddings that wouldn't benefit from a drizzle of raspberry coulis, and a hint of Kirsch or framboise just lifts it to the next level.

Makes: Approx. 250ml
Equipment: Food processor
Preparation time: 15 minutes
Freeze: Yes – freeze in small batches for up to 6 months and defrost at room temperature

350g fresh raspberries, or frozen and defrosted
25g unrefined caster sugar, or to taste
60ml water
½ tsp lemon juice
1 tsp Kirsch or framboise (optional)

Blitz the raspberries to a purée in a food processor.

Strain the fruit in small batches through a nylon sieve placed over a bowl. Press the fruit very hard with the back of a spoon to ensure you have all the flesh and juice squeezed through, leaving behind just the pips and skin.

Whisk in the sugar, water, lemon juice and Kirsch or framboise, if using, until the sugar dissolves.

Taste and add extra sugar, if preferred.

Serve chilled or at room temperature. Store in a sterilised jar in the fridge for up to 7 days.

DAMSON COULIS

This is the perfect accompaniment to my Traditional Manhattan Cheesecake on page 91.

Makes: Approx. 750 ml
Preparation time: 10 minutes
Cooking time: Approx. 30 minutes
Freeze: Yes – if, like me, you are lucky enough to live near a ready supply of wild damsons, forage as many as you can, then make a huge batch of coulis. Freeze the surplus in 200ml individual freezer bags, then you need only defrost enough for a single delicious dessert, keeping the rest for another time.

500g damsons
200ml water
125g unrefined caster sugar, or to taste

Put the damsons and water into a large saucepan and bring to a slow simmer. Cook gently, stirring occasionally, until the damsons fall apart and the stones come free.

Remove from the heat and tip the damsons into a metal sieve set over a large mixing bowl. Using the back of a large wooden spoon, firmly press the fruit through the sieve to remove the skins and stones.

Stir in the sugar. I like my coulis quite tart, but if you need more sugar, add to taste.

Leave to cool, then store in a sterilised jar in the fridge for up to 7 days.

SEVILLE MARMALADE RIPPLE

I love marmalade, especially the really dark, thick-cut variety, but it had never occurred to me to make my own until one miserable January afternoon I spotted some Seville oranges in my local organic shop. I knew these were only available for a limited time, and I thought Charlie and I should try making some marmalade. I hit the internet looking for quick recipes and found quite a few. Charlie and I dutifully chopped, blitzed and boiled, but 20 minutes later, the marmalade was full of pips and the chunky rind wasn't cooked. But it tasted really good. I rushed back to the shop and bought more oranges. This time I cooked them first so that the skin was nice and soft, and boiled the pips separately to release the pectin. I use this in puddings, on toast and rippled through ice cream. The recipe is for a small quantity, so double the ingredients for a bigger batch.

Makes: Approx. 1kg
Equipment: 3 or 4 jam jars;
food processor (optional)
Preparation time: 20 minutes
Cooking time: 2 hours plus
approx. 20 minutes
Freeze: No

350g Seville oranges
1.2 litres water
45ml lemon juice (approx. 1 lemon)
650g unrefined golden granulated
   sugar
50g unrefined soft dark brown sugar

For the Pips
100ml water

TIP *Seville oranges freeze beautifully so if you don't have time to make the marmalade when they are in season, just give them a good wash and a thorough dry, then pop them into a freezer bag and into the freezer. When you are ready to use them, don't bother defrosting them; just pop them into the saucepan and off you go.*

Put the oranges and water into a large saucepan and bring to the boil. Simmer over a very low heat for 2 hours, constantly checking that the pan doesn't boil dry, and topping up with boiling water if it does.

Whilst the oranges are simmering, sterilise the jam jars in a cool oven at 110°C/90°C fan/Gas ¼, for 30 minutes. Submerge the lids and a ladle in boiling water for 1 minute and place 2 saucers in the freezer.

Using a large slotted spoon, remove the oranges from the pan and leave to cool in a bowl. Reserve 120ml of the cooking liquid.

Cut the cooled oranges in half, remove the pips and set aside. If you have a food processor, blitz half the oranges in it until they are finely cut. If not, chop by hand.

Place the pips in a small saucepan with the water covering them. Bring to the boil for 5 minutes, then remove from the heat and strain, reserving the small amount of liquid and discarding the pips.

Put all the oranges into a large saucepan. Add the reserved 120ml cooking liquid, the lemon juice and the reserved pip water. Add both sugars and stir over a low heat to dissolve, then heat without stirring until it comes to the boil. Boil rapidly for 15 minutes, scoop some of the marmalade out with a large spoon, leave in the spoon to cool for 20 seconds, then turn the spoon onto its side over the saucepan. If it drips off in lumps, take the pan off the heat and take one saucer from the freezer. Place a tablespoon of marmalade on the saucer and leave for a couple of minutes. Gently push your finger through the marmalade; if it crinkles, then it has set. If not, return the pan to the heat and boil for a few more minutes before testing again with the second saucer.

Skim off any scum from the surface using a metal spoon. Leave the marmalade to cool in the pan for 10 minutes, then stir before ladling into the warm sterilised jars and sealing.

BUTTERSCOTCH SAUCE

I always make this a day or two in advance and store it in an airtight container in the fridge, which allows the sauce to thicken and the flavours to develop. If you want to serve the sauce warm, just gently reheat it in a saucepan.

Makes: Approx. 250ml
Preparation time: 5 minutes
Cooking time: 10 minutes
Freeze: Yes — pour the cooled sauce into an airtight container or ziplock freezer bag and freeze for up to 2 months. Defrost overnight in the fridge.

110g dairy-free spread
175g unrefined soft light brown
  sugar
275g golden syrup
225ml soya or coconut cream
½ tsp vanilla extract

Put the dairy-free spread, sugar and syrup into a medium heavy-based saucepan and gently melt over a low heat. Simmer for 5 minutes, stirring with a wooden spoon.

Remove from the heat and gradually stir in the soya or coconut cream and vanilla extract.

Return to the heat and continue stirring for 2–3 minutes or until the dairy-free spread has been amalgamated and the sauce is smooth and glossy.

Remove from the heat and leave to cool.

CREME PATISSIERE

Literally meaning 'pastry cook's cream', this is used as a base for all kinds of tarts and pastries. To ensure it sets perfectly and will hold your layers of fruit, you need to bring it to the boil and vigorously whisk for a few minutes. Don't be fooled into thinking it is ready just because it has started to thicken; boiling and whisking are key.

Makes: 450ml
Equipment: Electric hand mixer
Preparation time: 15 minutes
Cooking time: 30 minutes
Freeze: No

6 large egg yolks
100g unrefined caster sugar
25g cornflour
350ml soya, almond, rice or
    coconut milk
1 vanilla pod, split lengthways

Using an electric hand mixer, beat the egg yolks and sugar together in a large bowl until light and creamy.

Sprinkle the cornflour over the surface and stir to combine.

Put the milk in a large heavy-based saucepan. Scrape out the seeds from the vanilla pod and add to the milk with the pod.

Bring the milk to the boil over a medium heat, then carefully remove the vanilla pod.

Gradually pour the milk into the egg and sugar mixture, whisking constantly with a balloon whisk to stop it turning lumpy.

Return the mixture to the saucepan and, over a low heat, continue to whisk vigorously until it comes to the boil and starts to thicken. Keep whisking for a further couple of minutes.

Remove from the heat and pour into a bowl. Cover the surface (not the bowl) with clingfilm to stop a skin forming and leave to cool. Once cool, chill in the fridge until needed, for up to 3 days.

CHOCOLATE CREME PATISSIERE

This is a wonderful alternative to vanilla crème pâtissière that can be used as a base for tarts, or as a filling for cakes and pastries.

Makes: 450ml
Equipment: Electric hand mixer
Preparation time: 15 minutes
Cooking time: 30 minutes
Freeze: No

250ml coconut milk
1 vanilla pod, split lengthways
2 tsp cocoa powder
60g unrefined caster sugar
3 large egg yolks
25g cornflour

Put the milk into a large heavy-based saucepan. Scrape out the seeds from the vanilla pod and add to the milk with the pod. Add the cocoa powder and half the sugar.

Using an electric hand mixer, beat the egg yolks with the remaining sugar until light and creamy.

Sprinkle the cornflour over the surface and stir to combine.

Bring the milk to just below boiling point, then remove the vanilla pod. Carefully pour half of milk over the egg and sugar mixture, whisking constantly to prevent lumps from forming. Add the remaining milk, whisk to combine, then return the mixture to the saucepan.

Continue to whisk vigorously over a medium heat until the milk comes to the boil and starts to thicken. Keep whisking for a few more minutes.

Remove from the heat and pour into a bowl. Cover the surface (not the bowl) with clingfilm to stop a skin forming and leave to cool. Once cool, chill in the fridge until needed, for up to 3 days.

RASPBERRY RIPPLE

Whilst I love raspberries, I do find the pips really annoying, so this recipe is absolutely perfect for me and I use it instead of jam in lots of my puddings. It's quick to make, and because it works with frozen raspberries, can be made any time of year.

Makes: Approx. 200ml
Cooking time: Approx. 25 minutes
Freeze: No – store in the fridge for up to 1 week

400g fresh or frozen raspberries
80g unrefined granulated sugar
45ml water (if using fresh raspberries)

Put the raspberries, sugar and water (if using fresh raspberries) into a saucepan and slowly bring to the boil, stirring regularly to stop the sugar burning.

Reduce to a slowly bubbling simmer until the raspberries have broken down, about 10 minutes.

Remove from the heat and strain in small batches through a metal sieve into a bowl, pressing the fruit really hard with the back of a spoon to ensure you have all the flesh and juice squeezed through, leaving just the pips behind.

Return the juice to the pan and bring to a slowly bubbling simmer. Simmer until thick and syrupy, about 15 minutes.

Remove from the heat and leave to cool completely; the ripple will thicken as it cools. Store in a sterilised jar in the fridge for up to 7 days.

TIP *If you try straining the fruit through the sieve in one go you won't have room to squeeze the fruit as firmly as you need to. Squeezing in batches will ensure you get as much fruit in your ripple as possible.*

SALTED CARAMEL

Salted caramel is one of my all-time favourite flavours, so you can imagine how bereft I felt when I removed dairy from my diet. I know you can make caramel without adding cream, but it just doesn't have the depth of flavour I crave. Making your own can be daunting, so take it very slowly and don't get discouraged if you don't get it right straight away.

Makes: Approx. 560ml
Preparation time: 2 minutes
Cooking time: 30 minutes
Freeze: No

485g granulated sugar
125ml water
A few drops of lemon juice
2 tsp sea salt flakes
170ml soya cream

Sprinkle the sugar evenly over the base of a medium heavy-based saucepan and pour over the water, ensuring the sugar is evenly moistened and there are no dry patches. Dissolve the sugar into a clear syrup over a low to medium heat, without stirring. Add the lemon juice to prevent the sugar from crystallising.

Continue cooking the caramel until it starts to turn a golden colour, 15–20 minutes, keeping a good watch as caramel can burn in an instant.

Once it is the colour of a new penny, remove from the heat and very carefully add the salt and cream. The caramel will foam up so pour the cream in very slowly. Stir using a heatproof spoon. If it has gone a little lumpy, return to the heat and stir until the lumps have disappeared, then very carefully pour through a metal sieve set over a mixing bowl.

Cover loosely and cool into a thick sauce. Store in an airtight container in the fridge. To thin it, gently heat in a saucepan, taking care it doesn't boil.

FRANGIPANE
OR ALMOND CREAM

Recipes for frangipane have been found going back as far as the early 17th century, when they were commonly made from almonds or pistachios and referred to as custards. These days frangipane is used to fill pastries, tarts and cakes, and I love experimenting with different ways in which to use it. It makes a perfect base for fruit tarts, a wonderful topping for pies, and tastes delicious filling a tart all on its own with just a dressing of flaked almonds.

Makes: 450g
Equipment: Electric hand mixer
Preparation time: Approx. 15 minutes
Freeze: No

125g dairy-free spread
125g unrefined caster sugar
125g ground almonds
25g wheat- and gluten-free plain flour
2 medium eggs, beaten
1 tbsp Calvados, rum, or pear liqueur (optional)

In a large bowl, use an electric hand mixer to beat the dairy-free spread until nice and smooth, about 30 seconds.

Add the sugar and ground almonds and beat until combined.

Sift the flour into the mixture, add the beaten eggs and the alcohol, if using, and beat again until the mixture is nice and smooth.

Cover the surface with clingfilm and store in the fridge for up to 1 week. Bring to room temperature 30 minutes before using.

CRANBERRY AND PORT MINCEMEAT

I absolutely adore mincemeat, and in fact will almost go as far as to say it is my favourite Christmas foodie thing – almost! I spent years buying jars of it from the supermarket, upmarket delis and village fairs, until one Christmas a friend and I decided to make some to sell at the Christmas school fête. It was a hoot. We had carols playing in the background, endless cups of tea and gossip, and at the end of it we produced jars of the most delicious mincemeat. Needless to say it sold out and I have never been tempted to buy another jar since.

Makes: Approx. 1.3kg
Equipment: Selection of jam jars
Preparation time: 30 minutes plus overnight macerating
Cooking time: 3 hours

120ml cranberry juice
220g fresh or frozen cranberries
175g unrefined soft light brown sugar
2 tsp ground cinnamon
½ tsp ground allspice
½ tsp ground ginger
175g currants
175g raisins
175g dried cranberries
25g flaked almonds
115g wheat- and gluten-free vegetarian suet
1 large Bramley apple, about 300g, cored and finely chopped
70ml maple syrup
2 tbsp honey
Grated zest and juice of 1 medium orange
50ml Port or brandy

Put all the ingredients except the Port or brandy into a large ovenproof container; a mixing bowl or casserole work well.

Using your hands, mix the ingredients together thoroughly, then cover with foil and leave in a cool place overnight, to allow all the flavours to develop and blend together.

The next day, preheat the oven to 120°C/110°C fan/Gas ¼.

Place the covered bowl in the oven and leave for 3 hours.

Remove the bowl from the oven and lightly stir the mincemeat. It will look very runny and fatty, but as it begins to cool the melted suet will begin to set. Leave to cool completely, stirring occasionally, then stir in the Port or brandy.

Meanwhile, sterilise the jars in the oven, lowered to 110°C/90°C fan/Gas ¼ for 30 minutes. Plunge the lids into boiling water for 1 minute.

Pack the cooled mincemeat firmly into the jars, place a wax disc on top and seal with the lids.

Store in a cool, dry cupboard for up to a year.

LADY'S FINGERS

These sponge fingers are easy to prepare, and making your own means you can create any trifle that takes your fancy, or if, like me, you adore an authentic tiramisù.

Makes: 25 fingers
Equipment: Electric hand mixer; piping bag and nozzle
Cooking time: 10–12 minutes
Freeze: Yes – for up to 2 months

3 large eggs, separated
70g unrefined caster sugar
40g wheat- and gluten-free plain flour
½ tsp xanthan gum
40g cornflour
2 tbsp icing sugar

Preheat the oven to 200°C/180°C fan/Gas 6 and line 2 baking sheets with baking parchment.

In a large bowl, use an electric hand mixer to whisk the egg whites until firm, then gradually whisk in the sugar 1 tablespoon at a time until it is all incorporated.

In a separate bowl, lightly whisk the egg yolks before carefully folding them into the egg whites.

Mix the flour, xanthan gum and cornflour together, sift the dry ingredients into the meringue mixture and very gently fold in until nice and smooth.

Spoon the mixture into a piping bag fitted with a 1.5cm pastry nozzle (you may have to do this in 2 batches). Pipe a small blob of mixture onto each corner of the baking sheet to ensure the baking parchment doesn't slip. Pipe 8cm lengths onto the baking parchment, leaving a small gap between each to allow room for the fingers to spread.

Sift half the icing sugar over the fingers and leave to stand for 10 minutes before baking in the oven for 10–12 minutes or until they turn a light golden colour. Remove from the oven and leave to cool for a couple of minutes before transferring to a wire rack. Dust the fingers with the remaining icing sugar and leave them to cool completely before storing in an airtight container.

TIP *I place my piping bag in a tall glass and fold the top of the bag down over the rim, I then half-fill the bag before pulling the top of the bag up and gently twisting the top to make sure the mixture doesn't squeeze out of the wrong end!*

PRUNES SOAKED IN ARMAGNAC

Please don't be put off prunes because of their association with a certain gastric complaint, because these wonderfully boozy ones are absolutely delicious. Whilst I am more than happy to eat them on their own, they are truly magnificent served with their syrup over chocolate, vanilla or coffee ice cream, or as an ingredient in soufflés, tarts and tortes.

Makes: 500g
Equipment: Large storage jar, sterilised (see page 151)
Preparation time: 5 minutes, plus 1 week storing

45g unrefined caster sugar
375ml water
½ vanilla pod, split lengthways
500g large pitted unsulphured prunes
185ml Armagnac, brandy or Calvados

Put the sugar and water into a small heavy-based saucepan.

Scrape out the seeds from the half vanilla pod, then add the seeds and the scraped half pod to the sugar and water. Place over a medium heat, stirring constantly until the sugar dissolves, then bring to a boil.

Remove from the heat and leave to cool for 10 minutes.

Place the prunes in the sterilised jar and pour the syrup, including the vanilla pod, over them.

Leave to cool then pour the Armagnac, brandy or Calvados into the jar and swirl to make sure it combines with the syrup.

Chill in the fridge for a minimum of 1 week, then taste the syrup and add more Armagnac, brandy or Calvados if necessary. Store indefinitely in the fridge.

TIP *I make a big batch of these every November, dividing them into small jars mid-December to make wonderful Christmas gifts for friends and family. Remember to attach a label with storage instructions and suggestions on how to use them.*

HONEY-ROASTED ALMONDS

These deliciously crunchy and sticky nuts don't hang around long in our house; I sprinkle them over everything and anything, and have been known to add a few to my morning porridge.

Makes: 100g
Preparation time: 5 minutes
Cooking time: 10–12 minutes
Freeze: No

100g flaked almonds
2 tbsp runny honey

Preheat the oven to 180°C/160°C fan/Gas 4 and line a baking sheet with baking parchment.

Sprinkle the flaked almonds evenly onto the baking sheet and toast in the oven for 5 minutes. Keep a close eye as they burn easily.

Remove from the oven and leave to cool.

Pour the honey into a large heavy-based frying pan and heat gently for a couple of minutes until warm and very runny.

Tip the cooled almonds into the frying pan and stir well to make sure they are all coated in honey.

Pour the nuts back onto the baking sheet and spread them out as much as you can before baking in the oven for 5 minutes.

Remove from the oven and leave to cool completely. They will clump together as they are a little sticky, but you can break them apart if you like.

Store on a sheet of baking parchment in an airtight container for up to 1 week.

TIP *I also love honey-roasting whole almonds, pecans and hazelnuts: Roast 175g mixed nuts for 5–6 minutes, cool slightly then roughly chop and pour over 125g runny honey. Stir well and bake for 5 minutes before allowing to cool and storing in an airtight jar for up to 1 month.*

PEANUT BRITTLE

Sprinkle or layer through your favourite ice cream or use to top pavlovas and meringues – I just eat it straight from the tin!

Makes: Approx. 225g
Equipment: Food processor
Preparation time: 5 minutes
Cooking time: 15 minutes
Freeze: No

150g granulated sugar
100g roasted, salted peanuts

Put the sugar in an even layer in a medium heavy-based saucepan and slowly begin to melt it over a very low heat, without stirring, until it turns to a lovely liquid caramel. Keep a close eye on it because sugar is very easy to burn.

Remove the caramel from the heat, quickly add the peanuts and stir to coat them all. Tip onto a baking sheet lined with baking parchment and spread out in a single layer, then leave to cool.

Once cool, break into small pieces then, if you like, finely chop in a food processor.

TIP 1 Don't be tempted to use raw sugar or unrefined granulated sugar as both contain impurities that can inhibit caramelisation; only refined granulated sugar makes successful caramel.

TIP 2 Almonds and pecans also work here, and taste especially good, but toast them at 180°C/160°C fan/Gas 4 for 10–15 minutes before adding them to the caramel

Index

A

agave nectar 11
alcohol 8
almond 73, 102
  almond milk 118–20, 139, 146
  almond pastry 20, 29
  blueberry and raspberry amandines 38–9
  frangipane 'almond cream' 150
  honey roasted almonds 154
  macaroon and toasted almond mincemeat tartlets 29
  sour cherry and almond clafoutis 74
amandines, blueberry and raspberry 38–9
apple 58, 151
  apple sauce 52–3
  caramelised apple and pecan cheesecake pie 108
  Eve's pudding 79
  proper apple pie 52–3
  St Stephen's pudding 63
  tarte tatin 24–5
apricot
  apricot fool with orange polenta biscuits 98–9
  French apricot tart 42–3
Armagnac
  Armagnac cream 114–15
  chocolate, prune and Armagnac torte 102
  prunes soaked in Armagnac 153
avenins 10

B

baking powder 8
banana
  banana and coconut ice cream 132
  banana and toffee-filled brown sugar meringues with coconut cream and crunchy peanut brittle 104–5
  banoffee fools 103
  caramelised banana pie 51
bicarbonate of soda 8
biscuits, orange polenta 98–9
blackcurrant
  blackcurrant compote 106–7
  blackcurrant coulis 142
  blackcurrant ripple 48–9, 92–3, 142
  blackcurrant sorbet and mint shortbread sandwich 134–5
blueberry
  blueberry cream cheese tart 109
  blueberry and raspberry amandines 38–9
  little blueberry and vanilla trifles 110–11
bread pudding, coconut spiced 75
breadcrumbs 30, 58, 60, 62, 63, 76, 126
brown bread ice cream 126
brownie pots, hazelnut and Frangelico 80–1

C

caramel 113
  caramel sauce 108
  crème caramel 112
  salted caramel 148–9
  salted caramel sauce 103
cheesecake
  caramelised apple and pecan cheesecake pie 108
  espresso and hazelnut baked cheesecake 88–9
  quick and easy lemon cheesecake 92–3
  roasted gooseberry, ginger and elderflower cheesecake 86–7
  traditional Manhattan cheesecake 90–1
cherry, sour cherry and almond clafoutis 74
chocolate 8, 81, 88, 94, 103
  boozy chocolate, raspberry and coconut trifle pots 100–1
  chocolate, prune and Armagnac torte 102
  chocolate crème pâtissière 101, 147
  chocolate genoise 100–1, 111
  chocolate pâte sucrée 18, 34–5, 48–9

butterscotch
  butterscotch meringue tartlets 50
  butterscotch sauce 145

  chocolate sorbet 133
  chocolate walnut truffle tartlets with chocolate and Grand Marnier glaze 34–5
  dark and delicious chocolate syrup 138
  gingerbread soufflés 66–7
  hot chocolate soufflés 69
  pear, chocolate and hazelnut tart 26–7
  pots au chocolat with prune and Armagnac cream 114–15
  rich chocolate and hazelnut tart 37
  rich chocolate ice cream 120
  Scottish chocolate and hazelnut cranachan 70–1
  tarte tout chocolat 48–9
  warm and gooey chocolate fondant puddings 64–5
  see also white chocolate
Christmas crumble 82–3
Christmas pudding
  Christmas pudding ice cream 130–1
  my Mum's Christmas pudding 58
cinnamon custard 139
citrus custard 139
clafoutis, sour cherry and almond 74
Cocomega spread 9
coconut 8–9

banana and coconut ice
cream 132
boozy chocolate,
raspberry and coconut
trifle pots 100–1
coconut crema
catalana 113
coconut and rum
cream 75
coconut spiced bread
pudding 75
coconut cream 9, 10
banana and toffee-
filled brown sugar
meringues with
coconut cream and
crunchy peanut
brittle 104–5
coconut crema
catalana 113
for ice cream 121–3,
130–1
recipe 24, 30, 39, 57,
101, 103, 104, 111,
138
coconut milk 8–9, 75, 113,
118–23, 129–32, 138
coconut oil 8, 9
coconut palm sugar 11
coconut yoghurt 9, 10
coffee
coffee crème Anglaise
64, 139
coffee and Kahlúa ice
cream with mocha and
espresso ripple 121
mini pavlovas with coffee
and Kahlúa ice cream
and blackcurrant
compote 106–7
see also espresso
compote
blackcurrant 106–7
strawberry and
balsamic 40–1
coulis
blackcurrant 142
damson 143
raspberry 143

cranachan, Scottish
chocolate and
hazelnut 70–1
cranberry 58
cranberry and port
mincemeat 151
Lorna's cranberry torte
with orange, honey
and star anise
syrup 96–7
'cream'
Armagnac 114–15
coconut and rum 75
dairy-free 10
frangipane almond 150
see also coconut cream
'cream cheese', dairy free
10, 86, 88, 91, 94, 108
blueberry cream cheese
tart 109
crème Anglaise
coffee 139
rich and creamy
vanilla 139
crème caramel 112
crème pâtissière 26–7,
42–3, 146
chocolate 101, 147
raspberry crème
pâtissière tartlets
44–5
crumbles
Christmas crumble 82–3
rhubarb, orange and
hazelnut crumbles 59
custard 103, 111–13
cinnamon 139
citrus 139
Grand Marnier 78, 139
nutmeg and vanilla
custard tarts with
strawberry and
balsamic compote
40–1
rhubarb and custard
tartlets 28
rich and creamy
vanilla 78, 139

D
dairy free spreads 9
damson coulis 143
dates 57, 58, 97
dried fruit recipes 58, 63,
75, 151

E
eggs 9
elderflower, roasted
gooseberry and ginger
cheesecake 86–7
equipment 12–13
espresso 9, 81, 114
coffee crème Anglaise
64, 139
coffee and Kahlúa ice
cream with mocha and
espresso ripple 121
espresso and hazelnut
baked cheesecake
88–9
tiramisu 94–5
Eve's pudding 79

F
fats 9
flours 9
food allergies/intolerances 7
fools
apricot fool with orange
polenta biscuits 98–9
banoffee fools 103
Frangelico and hazelnut
brownie pots 80–1
frangipane 38–9, 43
frangipane `almond
cream' 150
gooseberry frangipane
galette 33
fruit 9

G
galette, gooseberry
frangipane 33

gelato
lemon custard gelato
with hot lemon sauce
124–5
Merlot gelato 128
genoise, chocolate 100–1,
111
ginger
gingerbread soufflés
66–7
roasted gooseberry,
ginger and elderflower
cheesecake 86–7
steamed ginger
sponges 60–1
glazes
apricot 42–3
Grand Marnier 34–5
golden syrup 10
gooseberry
gooseberry frangipane
galette 33
roasted gooseberry,
ginger and elderflower
cheesecake 86–7
Grand Marnier 126
chocolate walnut truffle
tartlets with chocolate
and Grand Marnier
glaze 34–5
Grand Marnier custard
78, 139
orange and Grand
Marnier soufflés 68

H
hazelnut 82–3, 107
espresso and hazelnut
baked cheesecake
88–9
hazelnut and Frangelico
brownie pots 80–1
hazelnut pastry 17, 37
pear, chocolate and
hazelnut tart 26–7
rhubarb, orange and
hazelnut crumbles
59

rich chocolate and
hazelnut tart 37
Scottish chocolate
and hazelnut
cranachan 70–1
white chocolate and
toasted hazelnut
ice cream 127
honey 10–11
honey roasted almonds
111, 154
orange, honey and star
anise syrup 96–7

I

ice cream
banana and coconut 132
brown bread 126
Christmas pudding 130–1
coffee and Kahlúa
106–7, 121
lemon custard gelato
with hot lemon
sauce 124–5
Madagascan vanilla 24,
30, 39, 57, 64, 81,
118–19, 126
Merlot gelato 128
peanut brittle and
raspberry 122–3
rich chocolate 120
walnut praline 52, 129
white chocolate and
toasted hazelnut 127

K

Kahlúa and coffee ice cream
106–7, 121

L

lady's fingers 94, 110–11,
152
lemon
lemon custard gelato
with hot lemon sauce
124–5

lemon meringue
tart 46–7
quick and easy lemon
cheesecake 92–3
tarte au citron with
caramelised crust 36

M

macaroon and toasted
almond mincemeat
tartlets 29
maple syrup 11
marmalade
chunky marmalade
sponge 78
Seville marmalade
ripple 144
meringue
banana and toffee-
filled brown sugar
meringues with
coconut cream and
crunchy peanut
brittle 104–5
butterscotch meringue
tartlets 50
lemon meringue
tart 46–7
mini pavlovas with coffee
and Kahlúa ice cream
and blackcurrant
compote 106–7
queen of puddings 76–7
Merlot gelato 128
milk products 9–10
milks, dairy-free 9–10,
118–20, 139, 146
see also coconut milk;
soya milk
mincemeat 82–3
cranberry and port
mincemeat 151
macaroon and toasted
almond mincemeat
tartlets 29
mint shortbread and
blackcurrant sorbet
sandwich 134–5

mocha and espresso ripple
with coffee and Kahlúa
ice cream 121

N

nut oils 10
nutmeg and vanilla custard
tarts with strawberry and
balsamic compote 40–1
nuts 10
see also specific nuts

O

oats 10, 70
oils 10
orange 128
apricot fool with
orange polenta
biscuits 98–9
individual rhubarb,
orange and hazelnut
crumbles 59
orange, honey and star
anise syrup 96–7
orange and Grand
Marnier soufflés 68
Seville marmalade
ripple 144
orange flower water
pastry 21, 28

P

pastry
almond 20, 29
hazelnut 17, 37
orange flower
water 21, 28
sweet shortcrust 16, 26,
30, 32–3, 44, 46, 52,
109
tips and techniques 14
see also pâte sucrée
pâte sucrée 18, 24, 36, 39,
40, 43, 50
chocolate 18

pavlovas, mini pavlovas
with coffee and Kahlúa ice
cream and blackcurrant
compote 106–7
peanut brittle 155
banana and toffee-
filled brown sugar
meringues with
coconut cream and
crunchy peanut
brittle 104–5
peanut brittle and
raspberry ice cream
122–3
pear, chocolate and hazelnut
tart 26–7
pecan
caramelised apple and
pecan cheesecake
pie 108
Charlie's pecan sticky
toffee puddings 56–7
perfect pecan pie 32
pies
caramelised apple and
pecan cheesecake
pie 108
caramelised banana
pie 51
perfect pecan pie 32
proper apple pie 52–3
polenta biscuits,
orange 98–9
port and cranberry
mincemeat 151
praline, walnut praline ice
cream 129
prune(s)
chocolate, prune and
Armagnac torte 102
pots au chocolat with
prune and Armagnac
cream 114–15
prunes soaked in
Armagnac 153

Q

queen of puddings 76–7

R

raspberry 70, 76, 128
   blueberry and raspberry
      amandines 38–9
   boozy chocolate,
      raspberry and coconut
      trifle pots 100–1
   peanut brittle and
      raspberry ice
      cream 122–3
   raspberry coulis 101, 143
   raspberry crème
      pâtissière tartlets
      44–5
   raspberry jam
      roly-poly 72–3
   raspberry ripple (sauce)
      148–9
rhubarb
   individual rhubarb,
      orange and hazelnut
      crumbles 59
   rhubarb and custard
      tartlets 28
rice milk 139, 146
roly-poly, raspberry jam
   72–3
rum 131, 132
   coconut and rum
      cream 75

S

St Stephen's pudding 63
shortbread, mint 134–5
sorbet
   blackcurrant 134–5
   chocolate 133
soufflés
   gingerbread
      soufflés 66–7
   hot chocolate soufflés 69
   orange and Grand
      Marnier soufflés 68
soya cream 10, 124, 127,
   145, 149
soya cream cheese 10
soya milk 118–20, 124–5,
127, 139, 146
strawberry and balsamic
   compote 40–1
suet (wheat- and gluten-
   free vegetarian) 10, 60,
   73, 151
   Jenny's syrup suet
      pudding 62
sugar 10–11
sweeteners 10
syrup
   dark and delicious
      chocolate syrup 138
   Jenny's syrup suet
      pudding 62
   orange, honey and star
      anise syrup 97

T

tarts
   blueberry cream cheese
      tart 109
   butterscotch meringue
      tartlets 50
   chocolate walnut truffle
      tartlets with chocolate
      and Grand Marnier
      glaze 34–5
   French apricot tart
      42–3
   lemon meringue
      tart 46–7
   macaroon and toasted
      almond mincemeat
      tartlets 29
   my treacle tart 30–1
   nutmeg and vanilla
      custard tarts with
      strawberry and
      balsamic
      compote 40–1
   pear, chocolate and
      hazelnut tart 26–7
   raspberry crème
      pâtissière
      tartlets 44–5
   rhubarb and custard
      tartlets 28
   rich chocolate and
      hazelnut tart 37
   tarte au citron with
      caramelised crust 36
   tarte tatin 24–5
   tarte tout chocolat 48–9
tiramisù 94–5
toffee
   banana and toffee-
      filled brown sugar
      meringues with
      coconut cream and
      crunchy peanut
      brittle 104–5
   Charlie's pecan sticky
      toffee puddings 56–7
torte
   chocolate, prune and
      Armagnac torte 102
   Lorna's cranberry torte
      with orange, honey and
      star anise syrup 96–7
treacle tart 30–1
trifles
   boozy chocolate,
      raspberry and coconut
      trifle pots 100–1
   little blueberry and
      vanilla trifles 110–11

V

vanilla 11, 112, 146
   little blueberry and
      vanilla trifles 110–11
   Madagascan vanilla ice
      cream 24, 30, 39, 57,
      64, 81, 118–19, 126
   nutmeg and vanilla
      custard tarts with
      strawberry and
      balsamic
      compote 40–1
   rich and creamy vanilla
      custard 78, 139
vegetable fats 9

W

walnut 97
   chocolate walnut truffle
      tartlets 34–5
   walnut praline ice cream
      52, 129
white chocolate 8, 44
   white chocolate and
      toasted hazelnut ice
      cream 127

X

xanthan gum 11

ACKNOWLEDGEMENTS

Oh my goodness, where do I start? There have been so many wonderful people with me on this beautiful book's journey, from my husband John and my son Charlie who believe in me, encourage me and love eating my puddings, to the fantastic staff at Quadrille who have produced a book far exceeding my hopes and expectations.

Thanks to Clare Hulton, my ever-supportive agent, who continues to show an amazing belief in my abilities. My gratitude to Anne Furniss at Quadrille who completely understood my passion and my enthusiasm for all things dairy-, wheat- and gluten-free and who introduced me to my wonderfully supportive editor Céline Hughes; your confidence in my recipes and my writing means a great deal.

Despite the intense summer heat, I had an absolute ball at the photo shoot, so my heartfelt thanks go to photographer Andrew Montgomery who produced the most amazing photographs, and to his family who allowed the team to camp and create havoc in their kitchen for one week last summer. To the creative director Helen Lewis and the incredibly talented designer Arielle Gamble, who took my somewhat convoluted vision for the book and improved upon it a hundredfold – my everlasting gratitude. Thank you, thank you, thank you to Emily and Natalie for baking and styling my puddings so beautifully; I am totally in awe of your speed, efficiency and talent. And although we never met, a huge thank you to Tamzin for understanding the feel of the book and sourcing such a wonderful array of props. And last but not least, thank you to Sally Somers for diligently dotting my i's and crossing my t's.

To all my family and friends who put up with me whilst I buried myself in baking and writing and who bravely tasted so many puddings – sorry and thank you! To my sister-in-law Catherine, whose kindness and generosity in providing me with a home from home in London made my rather hectic life so much easier – thank you so much and when can I visit next?! And to Marc, a massive thank you for your professional insights and for being such a great friend, and of course to Joe for gamely eating all the puddings put in front of him.

And last but not least, I want to thank my ever-growing band of customers and supporters who shared with me in the original Cake Angels story and who have now joined me in my new and exciting adventure www.juliaandson.com

Publishing Director: Sarah Lavelle
Editorial Director: Anne Furniss
Creative Director: Helen Lewis
Senior Editor: Céline Hughes
Designer and Illustrator: Arielle Gamble
Photographer: Andrew Montgomery
Food Stylist: Emily Jonzen
Prop Stylist: Tamzin Ferdinando
Production: Emily Noto and Vincent Smith

First published in 2015 by
Quadrille Publishing

Quadrille is an imprint of Hardie Grant
www.hardiegrant.com.au

Quadrille Publishing
Pentagon House
52–54 Southwark Street
London SE1 1UN
www.quadrille.co.uk

Cataloguing in Publication Data: a catalogue record for this book is available from the British Library.

ISBN: 978 184949 487 8

Printed in China

www.cooked.com

10 9 8 7 6 5 4 3 2 1